More
Haunted Northern New York

More
Haunted Northern New York

Cheri Revai

North Country Books
Utica, New York

MORE HAUNTED NORTHERN NEW YORK

ISBN 978-0-925168-94-8

Second printing 2005

Library of Congress Cataloging

Some of the names in the following stories have been
changed to protect individual's privacy.

NORTH COUNTRY BOOKS
311 Turner Street
Utica, New York 13501

With great affection,
I dedicate this book to my parents,
Tom and Jean Dishaw,
who taught me the power of the written word,
the importance of an open mind,
and the value of perseverance.

Contents

Part II - SPIRIT ENCOUNTERS WITH LOVED ONES

Acknowledgments

I'd like to thank all of the following people, in alphabetical order, for their assistance in writing this book. It's a bit of a cliché to say, "I couldn't have done it without you," but in this case, it's absolutely true. A book about people's experiences obviously requires the co-operation and permission of many people, so please forgive me if I've forgotten anyone:

Mark Anzalone, Steve Anzalone, Brent Augustus, John Bang, Gary Bartlett, Leon Burnap, Jeff Clark, Mahlon Clements, Megan Crowley, Ron Damon, Ola Demers, Joe DeVito, Sr., Margaret Gibbs, Jean Goddard, Diane Gusa, Robin & Jeffrey Hall, Kelly Jacoby, Ron Janowski, Hannelore Kissam, Nancy LaFaver, Charlie LaShombe, Frances Morrison, Trina Narrow, Jessie Olcott, Logan Thomas Patnode, Lisa Pitts, Sandy Putney, Diann Risley, Marie Rocca, Ann Sessions, Amy Shalton, Christopher Sharlow, Theresa Sharp, Chris Smith, Linda Stanley, Barry Strate, Susan Sweeney, Joan Szarka, Kimberley Trombley, Georgianne Muench, Karen Waid, Sandra Wyman, and Deatta Youngs.

The following individuals chose to remain anonymous, but they contributed as much as those identified above and I'm equally grateful:

Bob, Brian & Marissa, Carmela, Denise, Faith, Gloria, Jeremy, Jerry, Jodi, Julie T., Misty K., Misty, Pendra, Robert, Ruth E., Sue F., Steve T., and Wade.

I continue to be thankful to my dear family—Joe, Michelle, Jamie, Katie, and Nicole—for bearing with me, incredibly, through the crazy days and sleepless nights of a full-time working mother trying to write books on the side! And I thank Sheila Orlin, Rob Igoe, and the rest of the staff at North Country Books for their faith in me.

Much gratitude should also go to the people who read my

books—for their enthusiasm and loyalty—and to the book store managers selling my books who have become my staunchest allies. Special thanks to Robyn Kellison of Waldenbooks in Massena. Finally, I thank God for the many, *many* blessings He has given me, including all of those mentioned above.

Introduction

It's somewhat ironic that I'm writing the introduction to a book about a topic as chilling as ghosts in the sweltering heat of summer. Today is June 26, 2003, and here in the North Country—where we spit on glass just to see it freeze in the winter months—it's a whopping 91°, with a heat index of 105°! Talk about paranormal! And where are those ghosts when you need them to provide a sudden drop in temperature? I'll tell you where. All over Northern New York, on every street, in every town, in every county hardy enough to call itself part of the *real* North Country. That's where. It's a conspiracy!

No, I'm not paranoid (yet); although the heat may be getting to me. It's just that, ever since *Haunted Northern New York* came out, I've been deluged with ghost stories galore. People are coming out of the woodwork—people you would never expect it of—and they're telling their stories. The paranormal is becoming quite normal, at least in our neck of the woods. And this has made my work a lot easier.

When I wrote my first book, *Haunted Northern New York*, I went into it blindly—not having a clue what was expected of me as an author. I wrote about something I thought was interesting and trusted that there would be others who felt the same way. There were, and in a big way. Then, as I got into the signing and presentation circuit, I began to get some excellent feedback from readers. They told me what they wanted to see more of—or less off—and I listened. And when it came time to write this book, I took everything I learned into account and tried to give the readers exactly what they asked for.

Haunted Northern New York II covers a broader area than my first book. It ventures into Essex County with some incredible Adirondack ghost stories that have never been told in any other book. St. Lawrence, Franklin, Clinton, and Jefferson Counties are also well covered, once again, as they were in the first. Some of the stories include results of investigations and scientific corroboration of paranormal incidents. There's an entire section, in fact, devoted to Paraphysical Studies and Investigations (PSI), the people I recommend for investigative services. The majority of the stories are public, rather than anonymous. In fact, there are several Bed & Breakfasts that are sure to appeal to adventurers looking for that extra something in accommodations.

I again wove history into my stories as often as possible, and there are some real gems of history in the sequel that will blow your minds. I avoided "fillers" and legends and brought you stories with more substance. Each story I chose to use has something unusual about it; something I hadn't heard before—which is proving more and more difficult over time. And there are photos of many of the haunted locations, as well as some depicting spirit energy.

There is also a moving section about spirit encounters with loved ones who have passed over and returned to check in on their loved ones, or to bring messages from the other side.

I hope you enjoy reading the sequel as much as I've enjoyed writing it. Under normal circumstances, I might recommend grabbing a cup of hot chocolate and sitting in front of the fireplace at this point, before you begin to read this. But there's nothing normal about a 105-degree heat index in June in Northern New York, so a cold iced tea and a beach blanket might be more appropriate, depending on when you read this. Just don't mistake an approaching vaporous mirage of a person on the beach with a real bonafide ghost coming at you. Remember what I said earlier. They're *every*where!

PART I

Ghost Stories

A Rude Awakening

Norfolk

Photo by author
Home of Jeff Clark on the corner of Mill and Plumbrook, Norfolk

Andrea looked like hell when she walked into work one morning earlier this year. She'd obviously had a rough night. Her face sported a bruise and a scrape, like that from a rug burn. How could she tell her coworkers what happened when she didn't even know herself? How could she explain her suspicion that it was some psycho ghost living in her home that didn't want her sleeping there? How do you explain the unexplainable without adding insult to injury?

Jeff Clark bought the house on the corner of Mill and Plumbrook in 1989, but he now lives in Plattsburgh and rents the house out. Andrea has taken the brunt of menacing behavior from a disgruntled ghost or two in residence, since she and her boyfriend moved in last year. She confided to Jeff that she thought she might be going crazy because she was encountering some angry entities. He assured her she wasn't the only one to experience something strange in that house.

For Andrea, it began one night when she was lying in bed and woke to the sound of her bedroom door slamming shut. It takes a bit of force to shut the door—even for a grown man—because the carpet is so thick in the doorway that it impedes any movement of the door. Yet, that night, the door slammed so hard that it made the walls shake. Andrea said, "Who's there?" But all she heard was a low growl, like a rabid dog about to attack. She jumped out of bed and ran downstairs to tell her boyfriend, who had fallen asleep on the couch, to go up and get her son. Just as she was telling him what happened, she again heard the growling, only this time it came from the stairwell landing. The thing was stalking her! Her boyfriend ran up the stairs, but when he hit the top step, it was *freezing cold*, so he stopped right there and called to her son to come to the top so he could bring him down. Andrea refused to go back upstairs for the rest of that week.

When she finally did get up enough courage to sleep upstairs again, she wished she hadn't. That was the night she woke up on the floor, lying flat on her face with the sheet still under her, like she had been pulled off the foot of the bed by the sheets. The bed is built into an alcove of three walls, so the only way off or on is at the foot of the bed. It had been a rude awakening, for sure; and she had the bruise and carpet burn to prove it. Though Andrea has never been able to explain it, it's pretty obvious that some unknown presence upstairs didn't want her sleeping there that night, or any night, for that matter.

Another time she woke up to find a silver necklace that she never takes off lying on the pillow beside her head in a perfect circle, with the ends of the chain clasped, as if it had been carefully removed from her neck and laid out that way for her to find. Someone was playing games with her, but she didn't find it amusing. She also battled with the television, which seemed to have a mind of its own. It turned on, she shut it off, and the annoying exchange continued repeatedly until she finally gave up and let it stay on. Her daughter, who is only eight years old, isn't ready to give up just yet. She, too, has seen and heard a lot of things in the house, and she reported to her grandmother that there's always a cold spot at the stairwell landing, where her mother heard the second growl. However, instead of being frightened by it, the girl recently told the ghost and his dog to go away because they were scaring her mother. As of the time of this writing, that simple request from a fearless little girl seems to have worked.

Andrea and her daughter are not the only people who have experienced paranormal happenings in the house. During the eleven years of remodeling he did on the house, Jeff admits to hearing a male voice yell his name in the middle of the night a couple of times a year. He never thought much of it, until he started hearing stories from other occupants who had come and gone. One guy who rented from him said he always heard strange knocking when he was in bed that usually seemed to be coming from the attic. However, he did check the front door several times, and nobody was there. But he wasn't about to check the attic, and I can't say any of us would blame him. The same man once felt someone lie down on the bed next to him and thought it must have been one of his roommates; but when he opened his eyes and looked, there was nobody there—just an impression in the mattress as if someone was still lying there. By the time he jumped up and hit the light switch, whatever made the impression had gone, along with the impression itself.

Andrea said that she was never able to open the door to the attic, because it wouldn't budge. But one day when she was away, her friend managed to pry it open and brought some items up to the attic for storage. After that, they couldn't get the door to close. And that was also when things started getting nasty.

There are rumors of a scandal that took place when the house was owned by the keeper of the original gristmill on the property, who was probably also the builder and first occupant. The man allegedly had an affair with a local minister's wife, and when the minister interfered, someone ended up dying. Sketchy details at best. And not enough to point the finger at whoever might be haunting Jeff Clark's house. Some things are better left unexplained, like the bruise and scrapes on Andrea's face from a miserable old ghost.

A Tale of Two Tragedies

Moira

"Although it has been many years since they *lived* in the house their father built, two sisters may yet dwell in the shadows of an old Victorian house in Moira," according Ron Janowski, the current homeowner. Following is his story, as shared with me.

The Burnap House is a short walk from the center of Moira, a sleepy hamlet just west of Malone. In the summer of 1900, Charles E. Burnap, the son of a prominent Moira family, built the impressive home for his wife Mina, and their two young daughters, Margery, eleven, and Gladys, eight. His invalid mother, Esther, whom he had taken care of for almost ten years, would also be moving into the new house with her youngest son's family. At thirty-five, Charles was full of hope for the future and respect for the past. The house and a nearby meat market he built was his contribution to the rapidly growing community.

The house was built as a striking example of Queen Anne Victorian architecture, with an imposing tower, large rooms, a grand staircase, and stained glass windows. It represented the family's stake in the community and their uncommon good fortune. Unfortunately, tragedy marred that good fortune even before the Burnaps came to occupy the house.

When Moira's business district suffered a major fire that damaged many of the town's businesses, Charles' meat market was a near-total loss. As the family moved into their newly completed house in the early fall, however, things began to look up. They couldn't have known the most devastating tragedy was yet to come. On Christmas Day of 1900, the Burnaps hosted a party in their grand new home that was a huge success; and on Christmas night, the family went to bed in a jovial mood. It is impossible to imagine the horror that met them the following morning. Margery was dead. The cause given was "heart failure." Mysterious and tragic, their eleven-year-old daughter had died in her sleep. Her tombstone in nearby Sand Hill cemetery poignantly refers to the young girl as simply a "vanished star."

As terrible a tragedy as Margery's death was, life went on for the grieving family, as it has a way of doing. Charles' business flourished and home life was fine. For years, three generations of Burnaps continued to share the house. In June of 1911, the family celebrated Gladys' graduation from Moira High School. Gladys, vivacious and popular with her classmates, was the class salutatorian and had garnered a scholarship to prestigious Syracuse University. She had planned to leave Moira at the end of the summer, after visiting friends in the nearby Adirondacks. In late June, she left for a two-week visit to Tupper Lake. She would not live to see her home again.

Charles and Mina received word in early July that Gladys had fallen ill with a fever in Tupper Lake, and they left at once to be with her. Their only remaining daughter had contracted the dreaded "infantile paralysis" virus, or polio, and early on the morning of July 12, 1911, with her parents at her bedside, nineteen-year-old Gladys Burnap died. The distraught parents brought their daughter home for burial, but, because of polio's highly contagious nature, the sealed casket could not be taken into the house. Four days after Gladys' passing, Grandma Esther died in her bed, her heart broken at the loss of her "sunshine." Her casket was laid out beside that of her cherished granddaughter on the porch, a heartbreaking sight. Both were then buried beside Margery in Sand Hill cemetery.

Charles and Mina lived on in the big, empty house until Mina's death in 1940. Charles died 1951, when he took his spot next to his wife, daughters, and mother at Sand Hill.

The house, a silent witness to the past, remained, passing out of family hands shortly after Charles' death. It survived a typical history of sales and resales, apartment conversions, and bankruptcies, until the current owners acquired it in 1993. Ron and his wife Karen Waid, along with their son Philip, eight years old, fell in love with the magnificent home, and they have spent much of the past ten years restoring it to its original glory, often snapping progress pictures for their scrapbooks.

Photo by Ron Janowski

Apparition in the window of the Burnap House, Moira

In 1998, they found something unexpected in some pictures they had taken of the front of the house. In several of the photos, there was a figure in one of the front porch windows that appeared to be a young woman in a high-collared, Victorian dress standing inside the house and gazing out onto the porch. Ignorant of the home's history, the couple had no idea who the figure might be. A few years after the photos were taken, in the winter of 2000, Ron and Karen were in the front foyer when they caught movement out of the corners of their eyes. Above their heads—even though all of the doors and windows were shut and the furnace was off—the foyer's chandelier gently swayed back and forth. It continued swinging for a full five minutes. Between the mystery of the photographs and the swaying light, the

9

couple decided to find out more about their house's history. But it wasn't until the summer of 2003 that they actually did any serious research, and that was when they discovered the tragic history of the Burnap family. The pieces of the puzzle started coming together.

"Has Gladys returned to her beloved home to gaze out forever upon the porch where her mortal remains had rested shortly after her death?" Ron wonders. "And did little Margery return briefly on the 100th anniversary of her own mysterious death to signal her presence too?" It is impossible to say. But a woman who, as a child, had lived in the house years before once claimed to have seen a mysterious apparition of a young girl dressed in Victorian bedclothes in the house. The woman also claimed to have once been frightened by the spectral image of a 'bushy-headed man' who knelt down and attempted to speak with her.

During a recent visit by a guest sensitive to the spirit world, she spoke of several places around the house having 'strong texture,' and glimpsed the spirit of a man on the old servants' staircase in the back of the house who she described as a worker around the house. She said he was warm-hearted, friendly, and had a deep laugh. And completely unaware of the earlier reported sighting, she, too, described the man's appearance as bushy-headed.

"Today the house stands as a testament to the hopes and dreams of the young family that built it so long ago. But perhaps more, it may also be where the members of that family, along with others associated with the house's past, still remind the living that death may not necessarily be an end to our earthly existence, but merely a step into something beyond."

A Very Active Area

Russell

PSI, my investigative team, leaves no stone unturned when looking into allegedly "active" locations. Their methodical collection and analysis of information provides the basis for brutally honest reports. So if they tell me, after careful elimination of all scientific explanations, that they have a place that is likely to be experiencing genuine paranormal phenomena, I trust their judgment. And that's just what they told me about the area in and around the Town of Russell.

In *Haunted Northern New York*, I wrote about the Plumbrook Milling Company, an old mill that was once located in Russell. A bitter old miller is said to have been connected to the disappearance of Mary Millington, a pretty, young maiden who lived nearby. He loved her, she loved someone else; the miller couldn't face the cold truth, and the next thing anyone knew, they all came up missing. Then people started hearing strange noises coming from the direction of the mill, as if someone was still in the abandoned structure—still grinding stones, or worse, *bones*—and that was when the legend of the ghost of the Plumbrook Milling Company was born. I based the story I wrote on a very old newspaper clipping, but there was absolutely no documentation that anyone was aware of to support the legend, and no relatives were known to still be living to confirm its validity. PSI, however, came up with some very convincing evidence at the old mill site that actually *does* seem to support the legend.

According to John Bang of PSI, "The mill was an interesting place. We did get some electronic voice phenomenon (EVP) recordings of a man's gruff voice and what sounded like a young woman singing. This was mixed in with our own voices that were unfortunately carried across the plateau almost a hundred plus yards away. We also got a snapshot of the lower portion of the mill. In the picture were three orbs and a mist, with one of the orbs outside the mist. It was a clear, relatively dry night with little or no breeze and no insects. It was far enough away from residences to prevent contamination by most outside influences."

Photo by PSI
Three orbs and spirit mist at site of old Plumbrook Milling Company, Russell

John went on to explain that the atmosphere at that location provided highly favorable conditions for the detection of ambiguous energies. "We found the entire area to be super rich with silica and quartz deposits. As you know, these minerals are very conductive to various electrical and magnetic energies."

A man's gruff voice? A young woman singing? Three orbs in a mist? What more could I have possibly hoped for? You gotta love it when old legends are validated. And the PSI team didn't stop there. They said, "The whole area [of Russell] is known to be very active. In fact, one house, although well-maintained, has been boarded up, due to several potentially dangerous incidents involving paranormal activities. Fires and physical attacks have been reported by various people as recently as the 1990s."

They also visited another home on the Russell-Turnpike Road that was experiencing unusual activity. They took digital and film photographs of the house and grounds, some audio recordings, temperature and electromagnetic readings, and so on. What they found there was inconclusive, but when they brought in a trusted psychic to round out the investigation, she discovered a spirit belonging to a grandmother who was apparently still tending to the house.

Aggie

Morristown

In 1930, nineteen-year-old Agnes committed suicide by drinking liquid Lysol to escape her abusive father. Her mother died when Agnes was quite young, and she and her brother then suffered through many years of cruelty and neglect at the hands of their father. They lived in a large old house on Black Lake in the Town of Morristown. Agnes endured as long as she felt was humanly possible, but in the end, she chose death by caustic poisoning over life under her father's brutal rule.

Sixty-seven years later, Agnes returned in a flash. At least that's how Susan describes her—as a mysterious flash of light out of the corner of her eye. She first noticed it about a year after buying the house she had grown up in from her parents, who bought it from her grandparents in 1952. Susan, who has lived in the house for a total of about twenty-five years, was the third generation of her family to live there. Nobody, including herself, had ever noticed anything before in the house that indicated the presence of a ghost; but it soon become an undeniable fact that the house was, indeed, haunted.

Susan thought the strange flash of light might be a reflection in the windows from cars going by, but then she noticed that it was always near their open staircase, traveling up and down the stairs. One night, after two months of silently wondering what the light was, she began to ask her husband if he had ever seen it; but, before she could finish her question, he interrupted her with his own: "Do you mean the light going up and down the stairs?"

Assured that they had both seen the same thing, they were determined to get to the bottom of it. Closing the blinds easily eliminated the risk of reflections from passing cars. They realized that they might be experiencing something out of the ordinary. Their suspicions were confirmed when they started to see a young woman wearing a white nightgown on the stairway. Occasionally, they awoke in the middle of the night to see the same young woman standing in the bedroom doorway looking in on them. This occurred most often during difficult times in their lives. For example, when a close family member was very sick and about to die, the young woman began appearing in the middle of the night to each member of the family. She would always stand by their beds or in their bedroom doorways, looking quietly in at them. It was as if she was watching over them— the way she would have wanted to be watched over during her own unhappy lifetime.

The couple has noticed that when things were going smoothly and the family was content, their ghost—whom they endearingly call Aggie—appears less frequently, unless they are remodeling a room in the nearly 200-year-old home. Aggie always shows up when modifications are being made to the only home she ever knew. But even then, she is always a benevolent presence. Susan has never been afraid of Aggie—startled at times, but never afraid.

She says, "When I tell people about my ghost, they can't believe that I still live in this house. I obviously love this big, beautiful house as much as Aggie (or Agnes) does, and I have no problem sharing it with her."

An Alfred Hitchcock Thriller

Tupper Lake

In the 1970s, Jeannie purchased a duplex on Upper Park Street in Tupper Lake, and she and her children lived on the right side of the home. She was told that it had been a boarding house and that the top floors had been taken off. Nothing wrong with that. She was also told that it was where Grace Brown and Chester Gillette spent their last night together before he drowned her in Big Moose Lake the next day. That was a little unnerving. And there was one more thing she was told. A lumberjack who had been gambling at the house long ago and—I hesitate to even repeat this—was killed by someone who stabbed him up his nose with a pair of scissors. Now *that* was just plain disturbing, and so was the ghost, or whatever it was, that she would soon encounter in her bedroom.

About seven o'clock one hot summer evening, Jeannie had her young children take a bath and put on their pajamas before she took them out for a nice car ride to cool off and to get some ice cream. They returned home around dusk, and she put the little ones to bed, locked up, and got herself ready for bed. Two of her five children were lying in bed with her, watching TV. One of them, her daughter, fell asleep right away; so it was just she and her seven-year-old son, Michael, that were still awake. She said, "All of a sudden, beside my dresser on the right side, appeared a man, turned sideways to me. He was the same height as the TV on the dresser, had a houndstooth suit on, and was bald-headed. He looked just like Alfred Hitchcock. He never made a sound. He walked right out of my room and turned to the left and went down the stairs. He just went out of sight."

Jeannie had to hold Michael back, because he saw it, too, and he wanted to protect his mother. She didn't want to call her husband, a policeman, because they were separated at the time. But she was so frightened that she got the rifle, locked the bedroom door, and stayed up the rest of the night. The next morning at daybreak, she opened the door and looked in every room, closet, and all over the upstairs and downstairs. The "master of suspense" look-alike was nowhere to be found in the house, thankfully. When she was certain the coast was clear, Jeannie got her children up as quickly as possible and went to her mother's. In hindsight, she doesn't know why she didn't call the police or her parents to come over when the incident first occurred. She said she was young and didn't know what to do.

Unexplained shadows were often seen on the walls and ceilings of Jeannie's bedroom. But nothing could compare to her encounter with the man in the houndstooth suit. She said, "To this day, I don't know what we saw. It wasn't of this world, as far as I'm concerned." It was a terrifying incident that happened years ago, but she remembers it as clearly as if it were yesterday.

While many people have sought out the well-known Alfred Hitchcock cameo appearance in each of his movies, there are at least two people who hope they never catch another glimpse of his likeness as long as they live.

Beware of the Hand

Waddington

Carmela has had some bone-chilling experiences the past five years. In 1998 her family bought what seemed like the perfect home, at least at first glance. But they would discover, as many unsuspecting home buyers eventually do, that not everyone had moved out before their family moved in. In fact, it soon became apparent that there were not enough beds to go around!

The first few nights were deceivingly normal, according to Carmela, but then she started being awakened by something that made nightmares look like sweet dreams. She would be sound asleep, when all of a sudden it felt as if someone had jumped right on top of her and continued on half-way through her body! She couldn't move or even scream. She just lay there and waited for it to go away each time. This went on for three years.

Then one night in the summer of 2001, Carmela was asleep when the covers were suddenly ripped off her bed. She figured her sister or a friend who had spent the night was up to mischief, but when she marched downstairs to chastise them, she found them fast asleep, with the TV and the lights still on. At that same moment, she heard someone walk in and out of the back door—three times. She ignored it, thinking that it was her brother returning from another late-night outing. But when she didn't hear anyone come back inside, she went into the kitchen to investigate and spotted someone walking across their backyard. That confirmed her suspicion that it must have been her brother who was responsible for all the noise that she had heard since she was so rudely awakened just moments before.

The next morning when Carmela's mother came home from

work, she went to the counter near the back door where she always kept her purse so she could go grocery shopping, but her purse was missing. That was when Carmela realized that the noise she heard the night before coming from the kitchen was not from her brother; they had been robbed. And what's more, she realized that the same ghost who had scared her for three years by insisting on sleeping in her bed had actually tried to warn her that night by pulling her covers off and waking her up—but it was too late. Three other houses were hit that same night, and none of the stolen items were ever recovered.

After that, things settled down considerably, and Carmela found out that the ghost in her room was a woman. She was in the office upstairs one night talking to her boyfriend when she saw the figure of a woman in white walk by and go right into her room; then it came out and drifted into her sister's room. And that was the last that Carmela ever saw of her.

When Carmela's stepmother moved into the house later in 2001, Carmela moved out. You could say she moved out of the fire and into the frying pan; because, as luck would have it, Carmela once again found herself in a very haunted house. This time it was an apartment she shared with her mother. She believes there were three ghosts in the apartment—two men and a boy. The encounters started with the ghost of a very tall, slender man who appeared in her mother's bedroom doorway about six months after they moved in. Her mother screamed, with good reason, and the figure vanished. A few nights later, he came back, but this time he was not alone. There was another man with him. Again, he stood in her bedroom doorway staring at her; but at the same time, she felt a heavy hand pressing down on her.

The third time that the tall, male ghost returned to his customary spot in the doorway, Carmela's mother noticed the ghost of a young boy in the corner behind the man. The boy stared straight at Carmela's mother, but when she asked who he was, he turned around silently and walked straight through the wall, disappearing. The fourth and final time her mother saw anything was when only "the hand" that had applied the unpleasant pressure on her several nights before returned. This time, it appeared at the foot of her bed before it vanished into the mirror. Carmela's mother began spending her nights elsewhere, understandably, and she never saw the ghosts, or the hand, again. But that doesn't mean they were gone.

Carmela still heard tapping on the walls that sounded almost musical. She saw dark shadows moving around in her room at night, but she never witnessed any obvious apparitions like those that her mother encountered there. A month before both Carmela and her mother moved out of the apartment, Carmela was home alone watching a video and fell asleep around 12:30 a.m. A short time later, she was awakened by the sound of the TV being turned off, so she sat up and looked around, thinking that her mother had come home and turned it off. When she realized that her mother was still out, Carmela nervously turned the TV back on. That's when she noticed that the VCR had been turned off and the TV had been changed from channel 3 to channel 67. She knew that wasn't right, because she'd been watching a video when she fell asleep, and nobody else was home to change the channel or turn off the VCR. About two minutes after she turned the TV and VCR back on and put her movie back in, the TV turned off, then on, then off again. When she saw that it had returned to channel 67, she left the TV alone and stayed up until her mother returned.

A few nights later, Carmela rented Stephen King's "Rose Red," a two-video set. It's a lengthy miniseries about a paranormal investigator who takes a team of psychics into a haunted house. The ghost—the real ghost at Carmela's apartment—apparently didn't want to see how the movie ended, because when Carmela got to the second video, it was ejected three times from the VCR, as if the ghost was taunting her with an "investigate *this*" sort of attitude.

If you are a tenant in an apartment somewhere in Waddington, and your VCR is acting up, *beware*. It may be THE HAND!

Boo, Who?

Watertown

In 1987, Trina and two of her friends, Cathy and Kelly, moved into a modest two-story home on Alexandria Avenue. The first time Trina was completely alone in the house, she was in the kitchen doing dishes when she had the strong sense that someone had come up behind her. She thought they must have come in the front door and were going to try to scare or surprise her. She spun around and said, "Boo!" *Huh?* That was when she realized she had said "boo" to herself, which was somehow strangely appropriate. The idea that no one was there when she could feel a presence so strongly behind her was just plain creepy, and she decided she'd better leave for a while.

Trina often felt that someone was peering in at her through the kitchen window and the feeling was sometimes so strong that she actually grabbed a broom and ran out the side door, only to find no one there. She also felt cold "swooshes" go past her in the kitchen when no doors or windows were open. And she heard someone walking up the stairs toward her second-floor bedroom when supposedly nobody else was home.

The first time she heard footsteps, she thought it was Cathy; and, since she wanted to talk to her, she swung open the door to catch her friend as she went by. The hallway was completely empty. Cathy wasn't there, and, oddly, the footsteps stopped just as Trina opened the door. Other times when she heard someone walking toward her room, her kitten acted like she, too, had heard something. In typical cat style, she lifted her head, perked her ears up, and stared at the door like she was expecting it to open at any second. To this day, her aging cat still has a nervous temperament that began in that house.

Trina finally swallowed her pride about a year after they moved in and told her roommates of all of the strange things that had been happening to her. She was sure they would think she was nuts, which is why she waited so long to tell them; but Kelly reciprocated with her own share of unexplained experiences. She told Trina there had been times when she was awakened by a scratching on the window of her first-floor bedroom. The cat and kitten that regularly slept on her bed would stir and watch the window intently when this occurred. But each time Kelly got up to investigate, she found nothing. And she found nothing the time that she got up to investigate the loud, continuous banging on their old glass front door—a sound that neither of the other two roommates had heard. Finally, Kelly told about the time she awoke to the feeling of a heavy pressure on top of her, like someone was holding her down.

Shortly after their heart-to-heart about the strange occurrences, all three of the women moved out of the house and went their separate ways. One day Trina happened to be talking to a friend's mother who lives a few blocks from the house on Alexandria Avenue, and the woman was telling her about a suicide note they had found in the walls of their old home when they were remodeling. Apparently, a young man who lived in the woman's house had shot himself next to a bridge and culvert right behind the house Trina and her friends had rented. Trina thinks he may have been the restless soul that was haunting them.

She said, "He apparently still liked the girls (us, anyway), no matter what kind of personal problems he had that led him to suicide. It was a great coincidence that this young man once lived in the home that our friends now own. Their finding his suicide letter in the wall when renovating was how we learned of the suicide behind our rental house."

In dreams, bridges often symbolize the connection between the physical and the spiritual states. They can also be symbolic of crossing over (as from life to death) and are often reported by people who have had near-death experiences as a place they found themselves standing at while deciding whether to go toward the Light or return to their bodies. If the young man who committed suicide so many years ago is indeed the one who was haunting the rental property, I hope that he has finally crossed that bridge behind the house and gone Home.

#4 City Fire Station

Watertown

Courtesy of Neighbors of Watertown
Old #4 City Fire Station and Training Tower

Ron Damon was Fire Chief of the City of Watertown from 1981 to 1985, when he retired. He fought fires for more than thirty-one years and was the recipient of a medal for bravery. That may explain why his view of the fire station's ghost is a positive one, where others might think of *any* ghost experience as negative. The Chief has nothing but respect for the ghost or ghosts that reportedly have haunted the old station, and they seemed to feel the same about him.

The #4 City Fire Station was located on the corner of Lillian

Street and East Main Street on the city's north side. It had two bays, a training tower, and a smoke house that were built around 1910. When the station closed in the early 1980s, it sat vacant until Neighbors of Watertown, Inc. obtained it and converted it into six lovely and modern, two-bedroom apartments known today as Lillian Towers at 600 Lillian Street.

The ghosts appeared during the last couple of years that the building was used as a fire station, and for another year or two thereafter, when it was used only for record storage.

Sometimes the distinctive sound of a fireman walking in the hall and on the stairs wearing his boots was heard by a number of the firemen who were sleeping in the dorm. The big wooden locker doors were heard opening and closing every so often. In the mornings, after all the housework was done and everything was ready for inspection, locker doors were occasionally found opened, even though catches would not allow them to open by themselves. The men felt there was nothing threatening about the presence. They all matter-of-factly accepted that it was just the old-timers—firefighters of yesteryear.

One night when the men were in the dormitory, heavy footsteps were again heard on the stairs. The familiar sound of a booted fireman was climbing the stairs. The downstairs doors were locked, and the light from the watch desk at the bottom of the stairs cast only a faint glow. All of the men listened as the footsteps reached the top landing, turned into the hallway, and started down the hallway toward them. Determined to greet the ghost, one firefighter went through the bathroom and approached the hallway from the bathroom door, and another went through the center hall door at the same time and switched on the light. The sound stopped abruptly. The hall was empty. Yet, all of the men had clearly heard the footsteps that night.

After the station was closed down, it was completely secured. As fire chief, Ron had the only set of keys. One day he was there with the president of a nearby ambulance service looking for something in the basement. The doors were locked, and they were the only two people in the building. While in the basement, they heard someone walking overhead on the first floor, so Ron called up to ask who was

25

there but received no answer. He wasn't surprised. By then he had been hearing strange footsteps and listening to his men tell of similar experiences for quite some time, and he'd become used to it. At any rate, when he and the other man returned to the first floor, a quick inspection of the building confirmed that they were still the only ones there, and the front doors remained locked.

Another time, Ron and his wife and daughter went to the second-floor captain's office to find some paperwork. Ron was straining to see what was what in the shadows, because most of the electricity had been shut down when the fire station was closed. Suddenly, the "night lights" popped on. The night lights were a series of single-bulb ceiling lights throughout the station that could only be activated in two ways: by an incoming telegraph fire alarm box that automatically turned on the lights from a remote mechanism at the watch desk on the main floor; or by a manual switch, also at the watch desk on the main floor. There were no other light switches that could activate the night lights anywhere else in the building. But they somehow came on.

Of course, the family proceeded immediately to the watch desk to investigate but found that the doors were still locked and no one else was around. The switch had indeed been turned on, however, so Ron turned it back off. He wonders if a ghostly firefighter switched the lights on to help the Chief see what he was doing. A presence was definitely felt that night, he said, but it was friendly and respectful, like it knew he was the Chief.

Ron said rumors of the ghosts of the fire station have surfaced from time to time, and reporters have even called him inquiring, but he always declined to comment on it until now. He does not vouch for the ghosts or deny that they were there. He only points out that it's hard to explain some of the things that happened there in any other way.

Heaven on Earth

Upper Jay

Wellscroft Lodge Bed & Breakfast, Upper Jay

When Wellscroft Lodge first opened, customers were enchanted by the beauty of their surroundings, both inside and out. Guests commented on the charm of the soft orchestra music and how pleasant it was to hear people laughing and dancing gaily in the grand entrance below the guest bedrooms. It made them think of what it must have been like in days gone by, when it was a magnificent summer home used to entertain family and friends in the early 1900s. Wellscroft's proud new owner never knows quite how to tell her guests that the charming noises they hear that remind them of yesteryear might very well be the real thing.

Wellscroft was built as a summer home for Jean and Wallis Craig Smith of Saginaw, Michigan, in 1903. Jean's parents were natives of Upper Jay who became rich in Minnesota when her father stumbled upon a large iron ore mine, then wisely invested his fortune in the timber industry. The Smiths had Wellscroft constructed as an exact duplicate of a home they had fallen in love with in Scotland; hence, the English Tudor Revival theme. One of the largest Adirondack estates built in Essex County during that time period, Wellscroft was designed to be a self-contained retreat—complete with a caretaker's house, firehouse, power house, ice house, carriage house, maple syrup house, children's playhouse, golf course, stables, gardens, walkways, and more. The mansion itself was 17,000 square feet of remarkable architecture and décor, and the entire estate cost an estimated $500,000 back then—equivalent to about $10.5 million in today's dollars. Not bad for a mere summer home!

The Smiths vacationed and entertained at Wellscroft for several decades, until the stock market crash pummeled the family's fortune, and they could no longer afford to keep their beloved mountain mansion. In 1942, the property was sold and endured a number of changes in ownership over the next fifty years. There were periods when it was a private home, periods as a public resort bustling with activity, and periods of abandonment and neglect.

It was during a period of abandonment that Linda and Randolph Stanley happened upon Wellscroft, which is located at 158 Route 9N, about thirteen miles from Lake Placid. They had been scouring the region for a bed and breakfast that would provide both a place to retire in and a comfortable retirement income. Of course, the task of restoring the neglected and heavily vandalized estate to its original splendor was monumental, and it's still an ongoing process, as anyone can imagine. With their work cut out for them, the Stanleys won't have to worry about an early retirement, but I can think of no place I'd rather toil my days away than at Wellscroft. It's like Heaven on Earth, right down to the subtle intermingling of the physical world with the spirit world.

Linda showed me a stack of photographs she has accumulated

depicting Wellscroft through many of its former days, right up to the present. They've been invaluable in her endeavor to accurately restore the lodge to its original appearance. Some of the photographs show Wellscroft as it appeared when the Stanleys first bought it. One such photograph of the dining hall—remarkably undisturbed by vandals—shows an orb drifting across the ceiling; tangible evidence of the spirit activity believed to exist there.

Courtesy of Linda Stanley

This photo with an orb floating across the ceiling in the upper left corner was taken prior to renovation of Wellscroft by the Stanleys.

There is nothing frightening about the paranormal happenings at the estate. Most of the incidents are both mystical and mystifying. The music heard by guests has been described as soft, pretty, beautiful, and instrumental. It is sometimes heard at night, but the source of the music has never been found. In fact, at one point, before the new owners even had a radio on the premises, a visitor asked if they would mind turning the radio off. There was no possible source, at that point, for any music whatsoever.

Besides music, the sound of a group of people entering through the front door—all talking merrily at once—has been heard. The main door to the grand entrance is the original heavy door; and it's loud, creaky, and makes a very distinctive sound when opened. People have heard that particular door open, and then slam shut. One time when Linda heard it, she went to see who was there and found the door locked, as were all of the other doors to the mansion. One of her sons also heard it, and he said it was followed by the sound of people coming in. A painter the Stanleys hired also heard doors opening and closing one day when he knew every door downstairs was locked, and none of the doors were even *on* yet upstairs. He left that day and never returned. The unmistakable sound of one of the original old light switches clicking on has also been heard. There's nothing else that can duplicate that sound, and nobody was near it when it was heard.

Photo by author

Main door to grand entrance where ghosts are heard entering Wellscroft

Linda eventually called in a reader—a psychic who can sense the presence of ghosts and spirits. The first thing the reader said as he walked through the main door, was, "What is that room up there? You have a lady in a red dress who sits in the window watching for someone." That room was the "Green Room," or the "Spirit Room," as Linda now calls it, depending on who wants to know. The lady in red has also been "seen" by someone else, not known to be psychic, who visited the lodge before the reader had. That person said that they too saw a lady looking out the window of the Green Room. It may be the same woman a nine-year-old boy insists he saw floating down the grand staircase when his parents owned the place in the sixties. She had a Victorian hairstyle, and the reader said she "likes men." Linda has actually seen imprints on the cushion in the window when she cleans that room, as if someone had been sitting there, even when nobody has used that room since the last time it was dusted. And one person who tried to take a photograph of the Green Room had their camera stop working, just in that room.

Besides the lady in red, the reader also saw the spirit of someone wearing an unusual hat who lives in the yard between the old firehouse and the old powerhouse. Linda later found out that Frank, the

Photo by author
Grand staircase where boy saw ghost of "the lady in red" floating down

original caretaker, wore a strange, wide-brimmed straw hat, unlike any that the townspeople had ever before seen; he was easily recognized, mainly because of his unusual hat. Since he was known to keep Wellscroft immaculate, perhaps he's returned to see it authentically restored. It must do his soul good to see the fantastic job the Stanleys are doing.

The only other spirit discerned by the reader was that of a man on the third floor, standing with his arms crossed on his chest in a no-nonsense way in the doorway to the original men's servants' quarters. Originally, the third floor was used exclusively as the servants' quarters. The first owners must have thought the world of their maids and servants, because the quarters they provided them with would evoke envy in anyone, regardless of class. The walls, floors, and ceilings of the third floor are still lined with the original solid hardwood which remains in mint condition, and the views are beautiful. Linda Stanley believes there were some thirty servants working at the lodge when it was first built. For a servant, it must have been a dream job. No wonder one returned there after his death.

Though the main lodge is now fully restored with authentic European furnishings and is operating as a bed and breakfast, there are still other buildings and gardens to re-create and restore. One is the caretaker's cottage, which is a bit further up the mountainside but still in close proximity to the main lodge. The original structure of the caretaker's cottage burnt to the ground years ago. Amy Shalton, Town of Jay Deputy Historian, recalls being in the caretaker's cottage before it burned, and she said you could feel an unexplainable breeze go by sometimes when you were just standing there. She also remembered the immense peacefulness she always felt around the grounds.

She told me of an incident that happened to a previous caretaker's teenage son in the main lodge. The boy told her that he had been trying unsuccessfully to open a door in the kitchen area, but it wouldn't budge for quite some time. When he finally got it to open, he saw stairs leading down. Not wanting to go into the basement, he closed the door, only to find it then kept opening. First it wouldn't open, and then it wouldn't close; and what's worse, the stairs shifted direction. They were now pointing upward! Dazed, confused, and spooked, he went upstairs to find his mother who was cleaning. When they both came back down to the door, it was gone, and there was no sign that a door had ever even *been* in that spot. It was like something straight out of "The Twilight Zone." All they could find was a bare wall. It's possible that the young man was disoriented in such a large building with so many doors and nooks and crannies. However, he emphatically insisted that he knew exactly where that spot was. An enchanted stairway in a house overflowing with mystery.

Aside from an occasional unexplained incident such as that, Wellscroft truly is a marvel to behold, and it's easy to see why it was recently added to the National Historic Register. Every room is magnificent, and no expenses were spared to ensure a comfortable stay that is fit for a king.

It's not hard to see why people return again and again to Wellscroft. In fact, Linda Stanley jokes that she thinks she was a maid there in a previous life—then, more seriously, she adds that she wants her last stop in this life to be in the cemetery at the bottom of the drive, and she plans to come back and haunt Wellscroft herself. After visiting Wellscroft, it's easy to understand her devotion to the property.

If you ever stay there, there are no guarantees that you will see or hear anything unusual in a paranormal sense; but if you want the best chance of seeing "the lady in red," be sure to request the Green Room suite.

Hell Hath No Fury

Evans Mills

Evans Mills is a very small town with a very big problem—a ghost with a bad attitude. A long time ago right there on North Main Street, in a big old Victorian house, a teenage girl named Anne was supposedly stabbed to death by her own brother as her parents watched. They had found out she was practicing witchcraft, it is said, which was forbidden and sinful in the days of old. But that didn't justify her murder, and she is evidently determined that someone is going to pay for the crime, even if they had nothing to do with it.

The day Misty moved into her husband Mike's apartment, she was sitting downstairs with him, smoking a cigarette, and he handed her a metal ashtray. It was solid metal with no sharp edges, so she was taken aback when her hand got cut by it and started to bleed. She didn't dwell on it, though—it was just one of those strange things that happen—but then the same ashtray flew straight at Mike's head. That was when he told her it would be best if they quickly went upstairs to the living room. She didn't question him at the time. After all, he had been living there for a while before she moved in, and she was the newcomer. But it was not a very warm welcome.

From day one, Misty suffered from sweating and nightmares in the house. She was overwhelmed by a sense of dread and refused to stay in there alone. A week after moving in, she and Mike were on their way out to visit a friend when they realized they'd forgotten their cigarettes inside. While Misty stood in the doorway just off the hallway, Mike went on ahead and turned on the light. Just then, he was thrown backwards into the hallway and hit the kitchen floor. He jumped up and yelled at Misty, "Get the hell out of the house. Go!

Go! Go! Go!" He literally pushed her down the stairs toward the out-side door. On the way down, Misty heard a "very strange noise" that scared her. Once outside, she demanded to know what was going on. That was when Mike told her there was "something in his house, and it wasn't nice."

When the young couple returned home that evening, Misty stayed close by Mike's side, and they tried to go straight to bed, but things started falling off the wall. They decided they had better just leave again and let the ghost named "Anne" cool down—she had a very hot temper. When they returned the next morning, they tried to act as if nothing had happened; they cleaned up the house and invited some friends over. That was a mistake. The television kept switching channels to soap operas all by itself, and it wasn't long before every one of their guests had found a different reason to leave. But chang-ing channels was nothing compared to the bizarre incidents that were yet to come.

One day Mike's mother stopped by. It had been a horrible day, and the couple and she decided they were going to visit Misty's brother. Misty came out of the bathroom and went down the hallway into the kitchen. When she turned around to go back down the hall-way, there were hundreds of maggots blanketing the carpet in the hall. They were crawling out of the floorboards faster than anyone could clean them up. Mike's mother told them to go ahead without her, and she would clean up the mess, bravely disregarding the nature of the infestation. When the couple returned, there was no sign of mag-gots anywhere to be found—it was like they had never been there.

When Mike's brother's fiancee slept over one night, she had a dream in which she was transported back in time to Anne's murder. She witnessed the whole, bloody incident and woke up screaming. She and Mike's brother left right then and never even said goodbye.

Misty also experienced the awful murder, but in a different way. Before she was ever told of Anne's tragic murder, Misty felt horrible, sharp pains in her abdomen where Anne may have been stabbed. And Mike, who has been seeing spirits and ghosts since he was five, saw the bloodbath of the murder almost every time he walked up or down the stairs. In fact, the red blood stains from the actual murder were still on the stairs, and nobody has been able to get rid of them.

Mike's mother decided she would stay in the apartment when Mike and Misty moved to Alexandria Bay for seasonal work. At the time. She didn't mind Anne that much, and Anne didn't seem to mind her, until the broom incident.

One time when Mike's mother was cleaning the house, she found that the door to her room wouldn't open, so she propped a Wiccan broom up against it to supposedly keep the spirits out. Instead, it infuriated the ghost, who struck the poor woman forcefully in the leg with it. The resulting bruise lasted for more than a week. Mike's mother doesn't live there anymore, and neither do Mike and Misty.

The night they were to move out of the house was the worst night Misty remembers. Apparently the she-ghost was furious that Mike was leaving her for Misty. Buckets, ashtrays, and glasses of water were all thrown across the rooms of the apartment by unseen hands, and the ghost actually scratched Mike from the top of his back to the top of his pants. They quickly got out of the house, but they had to break into their new apartment, because the ghost had presumably stolen the key out of Mike's pants pocket. When they returned to the house in Evans Mills the next morning, the key was set precisely on the china cabinet, tauntingly in plain view.

No one has been able to get rid of Anne yet either, as far as we know. She seems to have no desire to leave until justice is served. But how can that happen when all of the players of the original death scene have long since passed away? You can't go on forever hating every soul that walks through the doors of your home, can you? If you're a ghost, you can, because hell hath no fury like a vengeful young woman murdered in cold blood.

Kappa Delta Sigma House

Canton

Kappa Delta Sigma House, Canton. Second-floor window on right side is where "Elaine" is said to have hung herself in the closet.

The "cold dorm" is a massive room jam-packed with bunk beds on the second floor of the KDS sorority house at 53 Park Street. The windows in the cold dorm are kept cracked open year-round for ventilation, so there's always a slight chill in the air; hence, the name, "cold dorm." One night not too long ago, a downright *bone*-chilling incident occurred in that room, when an apparition the sorority sisters named "Elaine" made a brazen appearance.

There is a legend, and it's not proven in any way as of yet, that a woman named Elaine hung herself in a bedroom closet on the second floor in the front right corner of the home. The story goes that Elaine was stood up at the altar, returned home in her wedding gown, and hung herself in the closet. Nobody knows when the legend originated or where the name of Elaine actually came from, but there does seem to be *some*one watching over the girls in the home.

Many of the girls have had the phone go dead when they are talking to boys who they later concede were not deemed acceptable by Elaine. If the boy is not right for the girl in the house, the big tip-off comes when the phone goes dead. If a boy *is* considered suitable for one of the girls, Elaine has ways of getting the young couple together. She doesn't intend to let another girl in *her* home be devastated by a doomed relationship with the opposite sex, like she was.

One girl became annoyed when her computer screen kept scrolling down to an old boyfriend's name when she was on AOL instant messenger one day. Every time she tried to continue typing, it scrolled back down to the same guy's name—a guy she hadn't spoken to in some time. She finally broke down and called her ex— and it should be noted that the phone line *did not* go dead. The young man said he had nothing to do with her computer's misbehavior, but the two of them decided to get together again at that point, and now they are married!

According to Megan Crowley, the Vice President and House Historian at the KDS house in 2002, the rumors of Elaine's ghost have kept the boys who visit the home on their best behavior, which is a good thing. She said they speak respectfully in the presence of the sorority sisters and especially in any conversation regarding Elaine. They don't want to be added to her blacklist!

The "bone-chilling incident" in the cold dorm happened when one young woman was awakened to the sound of another sister sobbing. She didn't ask her at the time what was wrong, because talking is forbidden in the room. Once you walk through the door, the only thing you're allowed to do is sleep; thus, ensuring there's always a silent area of the house conducive to a good night's sleep. However, the next morning at breakfast, the young woman anxiously asked the girl who sleeps on the top bunk of the first bed as you enter the room why she had been so upset the night before. The girl replied that she hadn't even slept at the house that night—she'd been somewhere else and had just gotten home that morning. Yet the sister who heard her crying also saw what she believed was her silhouetted form under the blankets of the bunk in question. In retrospect, it sounded like something a heart-broken Elaine might have been responsible for.

I was recording our conversation on a new, mini-tape recorder while Megan gave me the tour of the house. When we got to the room where Elaine is said to have hung herself, Megan was explaining how she sometimes scares herself while recounting the stories about Elaine to others. On my way home, I played back the tape to make sure I got it all. The very section of the tape where Megan said she scares herself—as we stood in Elaine's old room—came out very garbled, like an old tape about to break or how a tape sounds when the batteries begin to die. But the tape and the batteries were brand new. In fact, they were so new that I still had extra batteries from the package right in my car. So I pulled off and changed the batteries and tried again, but that section of the tape remains impossible to understand—just like the strange occurrences blamed on Elaine at the KDS house.

For that matter, it's just like the strange occurrences blamed on ghosts all over the North Country. They often remain impossible to understand.

Liberty Avenue II

Massena

Lisa and Charlie had barely settled in for the night when a strange tapping came over the baby monitor on Lisa's nightstand. It sounded like someone was tapping on the dresser in the baby's room where the monitor sat. Charlie jumped out of bed and ran across the hall to the nursery to see what was going on. The room was noticeably cooler. Then, just as he felt someone touch him on the shoulder, he realized that his newborn daughter, Belle, had stopped breathing in her crib!

Had the infant not roused from her father's frantic touch at that very moment, she might have succumbed to Sudden Infant Death Syndrome (SIDS), also known as crib death. The couple thanked God that Belle was okay, but who could they possibly thank for alerting them to their daughter's potential brush with death? They hadn't *seen* anyone, but they surely had heard Belle's rescuer tapping on the dresser over the monitor, and Charlie had felt the hand of the unknown guardian on his shoulder. It would be the first of many unexplained occurrences in the home.

Lisa and her young son, Jeff, moved into the apartment building on Liberty Avenue in 1997. After her wedding in 1999, her husband Charlie joined them, and in February 2000, little Belle came along. Two weeks before the baby's birth, Charlie's Uncle Barlow had passed away. Today Charlie wonders if perhaps it was the spirit of Uncle Barlow or his grandmother, Isabelle, who watched over their daughter in her first vulnerable months of life.

One year when Charlie's son, Eddie, was visiting at Christmastime, he was drifting off to sleep on the couch when he felt someone looking at him. He bolted up and, sure enough, saw someone watching him in the doorway to the kitchen from the dining room. Another time when Eddie saw an apparition in the doorway, he automatically asked for its name, rank, and serial number—something he was trained as a marine to do—and he warned the ghost that he had a gun pointed at it, at which time the ghost disappeared. Charlie and Lisa told him "it was nothing," a phrase they'd been using a lot.

If movements were heard upstairs when nobody was up there, Lisa would tell herself it was nothing. When the couple came home and found their outside doors wide open, even though they were sure they had closed and locked them, they'd agree that it was nothing. Every time Charlie went to answer the knocking at the front door and found nobody there, he'd say it was nothing. But eventually all of the nothings began to add up to *some*thing, defying a basic law of mathematics, not to mention the laws of physical science.

Things were getting more difficult to ignore and more impossible to brush off as "nothing." Lisa woke up one night when she felt someone sit down on the foot of her bed. With her eyes still closed, she sleepily asked the perpetrator, "What do you want?" Nobody answered, of course, because nobody was there. Her husband was at work, and the children were nestled all snug in their beds. And you can be sure Lisa did not have visions of sugarplums dancing in her head after that incident!

On very calm nights, the swing on the porch sometimes moved back and forth on its own. Items often disappeared immediately after being set down, only to be found days later in the very locations they had disappeared from. When the apartment adjacent to theirs was vacant, Charlie and Lisa both heard people in there every day. They heard them walking up and down the stairs and running along the wall, which was on the other side of their couch. Even when they were the only tenants in the entire apartment building, they still heard people walking or running around in the adjoining apartment; and—friendly ghost or not—Lisa admits it made their skin crawl.

Before the family moved out earlier this year, Lisa took pictures of the apartment as proof that it was in good repair and clean when they left. At the last minute, she decided to take a picture of the basement. When she had the film developed a short time later, she found several spirits in the last picture she took. The first spirit that she noticed was "very prominent," but it may have been a camera strap, strand of hair, or some other sort of interference unknown to the photographer that was on the lens when the photo was taken. Of course, it might also have been genuine spirit energy zipping past the camera when the photo was taken. The other anomalies can't be attributed to scientific explanations as easily. One image looks like a blue energy trying to manifest into an apparition, and another looks like a spirit wrapped in an American flag.

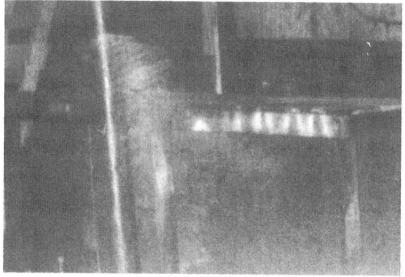

Photo by L. Pitts
Apparition taking shape in basement of Liberty Avenue apartment, looks as if arm is reaching out toward center of photograph.

Lisa and Charlie have not been the only tenants of the apartment building to notice that it was haunted. The people currently living in the end apartment said they have had things appear in pictures they took that were not there when they took them. They, too, will be moving out soon. Another previous tenant said that she felt things on her bed, like someone was sitting there and then got up. She also had been awakened by her bed shaking when she was alone.

Over the years, many tenants have been seen moving in and out of the building on Liberty Avenue, but it would seem there are a number of *unseen* tenants who have remained there through it all.

Liberty Avenue III

Massena

The house Misty lived in on Liberty Avenue is a tall, white, single-family dwelling—a nice-looking older home. She recalls a very cold winter day when her father had to jam a butter knife between the front door and the door frame, because the door wouldn't stay shut. There was nothing paranormal about it not staying shut; it just didn't hang evenly. But shortly after her father had secured the door to keep out the draft, the family was in the kitchen getting dinner ready when they heard Misty's grandfather yelling from the living room. He had been watching television when he felt a sudden rush of cold air. Somehow, the butter knife had dislodged from the front door and landed in front of the kitchen door, several yards away. It was bewildering to the family, because it would have taken some effort for anyone to pull the knife out, and nobody there had done it. That was when things really started getting chilly.

When Misty's family was away on vacation, they gave the house key to a trusted friend who would stop by once a day to feed their animals. As soon as they returned, Misty's mother went down in the cellar to do what every mother dreads doing the second she gets home from vacation—the laundry. When she lifted the washer lid, she was surprised to find that it was already full of warm water, as if someone had just been there and was trying to help out. She called her friend who took care of their pets, but the woman denied ever being down in the cellar. She only stopped in long enough to feed the animals, then left. Another unsolved mystery.

Misty also recalls many instances of hearing footsteps overhead on the second floor and in the attic, and she said people could be heard talking, but it sounded like they were actually "in the walls." Pet goldfish turned up missing, only to be found later in the basement.

After her parents' divorce, Misty moved into a new home and said she thinks that whatever was on Liberty Avenue may have followed her. A plant that hangs in front of a window over the kitchen sink sometimes starts swinging or spinning, even though the windows and doors are shut, and there's no breeze in the room. And her dog sometimes stands in the corner barking and jumping for no reason. Maybe it also sees the dark figures Misty sees walking by and the movement she catches out of the corner of her eye that is gone when she looks again. Misty has also felt the foot of her bed shake as she falls asleep. She has plenty of reasons to believe she's been followed.

Some areas seem to have a higher concentration of paranormal activity than others, and I would have to say that Liberty Avenue in Massena is such a place. In *Haunted Northern New York*, I spoke of "The House on Liberty Avenue," and this book includes two more stories from that same street. Another cluster of haunted homes is on the North Racquette River Road in Massena. Besides the obvious graveyards and battlefields, it makes you wonder what it is about certain locations that cause them to be more haunted than others.

Never Alone

Massena

Haunted home on North Raquette River Road, Massena

Jen and Scott moved into their house on the North Raquette River Road in August of 1998. Four months later, they discovered that they weren't the only ones living there. Not by a long shot. That's where their story begins.

Jen often stayed up working on crafts after the rest of the family had gone to bed. Scott's work as a supervisor required that he leave for work at 2 a.m., so he went to bed about 8 p.m.—the same time as the children. This gave Jen her much needed quiet time to get things done, uninterrupted. She usually went to bed by 11 p.m. Three or four times a week, she felt a light tap on her shoulder or back shortly after falling asleep, or just as she was falling asleep. She always opened her eyes expecting to see one of her sons. Instead, she saw a "faded figure, grayish-colored but with a glow" leaving the bedroom. Unsure of what to make of it, she kept the recurring incidents to herself.

A few times she got up and followed the figure out of her room and into her son Ian's room. There she watched as Ian said, "Let me go to sleep! I don't want to play anymore." Several other times she heard Ian talking in his room, and when she entered, she found him sitting up in bed, carrying on a conversation with someone she couldn't see. It always happened between 9 p.m. and 1 a.m.

At first, Ian denied the seemingly one-sided conversations Jen had observed when she questioned him about it. However, it wasn't long before he explained to her what was going on in his room. He had been talking to someone and playing pretend games with the unseen visitor, and his description of what was occurring matched what Jen saw whenever she peeked in his room. Interestingly, some of her son's board games that normally are kept in his toy box are occasionally found in places where they've never been placed by anyone in the household.

Jen also began to see the strange figure floating from one room to the next as she sat on the couch looking down the hallway. She wondered if lack of a decent night's sleep was causing her mind to play tricks on her. But one night, Scott, who was on disability for a work-related accident at the time, saw the figure right when Jen did. They were both sitting in the living room reading when they glanced up and saw the figure float by. Jen noticed Scott staring at her, and then he said, "Did you see that, or am I on too much pain medicine?" At that point, Jen decided to share it all with him. He confided that he, too, had been seeing the figure for a few months, but he thought he had been hallucinating.

From then on, they saw the figure—which they felt to be a "her"—nearly every night. The couple describes the apparition as faded, on the smaller side, with indistinguishable features and just enough visible matter to be able to tell that *some*thing is moving across the room. Another son has seen the apparition, as well, but describes it as slightly taller than what his parents think and said it looks like a thick cloud moving down the hallway. The boy has also seen a ghost-dog out of the corner of his eye, which he thinks is his dog, "Patches." He said he has also seen a feline apparition that possessed the same faded quality as the human apparition seen so often in the living room and hallway. Jen admits that she, too, has heard what sounds like their old dog barking somewhere in the house. Whether the animals are the family's lost pets or someone else's is not certain, but a psychic who visited the home told them that there was the spirit of an old man, a cat, and a dog that still live in the home. Jen believes there may be even more than that.

Jen used to fall asleep on the couch and be awakened by the sound of children playing nearby. She heard balls rolling across the floor and children running. The thermostats in the hallway were turned up to 90° some nights, even in the middle of the summer; Jen or Scott would turn them down several times throughout the wee hours, only to find them turned all the way back up to 90° in the morning. Other temperature anomalies in the house occurred in one of the boys' rooms just off the hallway. He was always extremely cold and needed more blankets, even when the entire house was warm and toasty. Whenever he gets the feeling that he is being followed around the house, it is always accompanied by a noticeable chill in the air immediately around him. Jen often feels the same way.

When Jen is talking on the phone to one of her friends who knows about the haunted happenings in their home, her friend will sometimes interrupt the conversation and ask Jen if she just noticed the apparition go by. It seem that at the same time that Jen sees a quick glimpse of their "shadow" ghost crossing the room, her friend hears a burst of interference on the other end of the line, unbeknownst to Jen. An interesting and quite accurate correlation can be drawn between the sightings and the sound of static.

Nighttime hasn't been the only time strange things have happened. Many mornings Jen makes her way to the kitchen to make coffee and finds the salt and pepper shakers tipped over on the stove. Her oldest stepson said he heard them and sometimes actually saw them fall. The door to the bathroom has opened when someone was taking a shower. At first it was only happening to Ian, and Jen and

Scott would hear him ask who it was. They thought he must not have closed the door all the way. Then it began happening to Jen and Scott. Jen tried locking the door, because it happened every time she was in there, but then she heard knocking on the door until she unlocked it.

Their ghost never wants to be alone, it seems, because it often hampers Jen's efforts to leave the house, like the time when she was home alone and getting ready to leave. She turned on the curling iron and left the bathroom for a few moments while it heated up, and when she returned to the room, she found it on the floor, turned off. Another time she was looking for her earrings that she always places on top of her dresser, and after much wasted time, they were found in one of the unused bottom drawers of the bathroom cabinet.

Jen says she never feels alone in their home, and the rest of the family concurs, as do friends and visitors. Their daughter says she always feels like she's being watched; and the boys say they often hear someone walking across the floor of the attic when they are home alone. A little girl Jen occasionally watches has been found waving at something in the hallways several times. One time, she was sitting in her highchair, then suddenly turned toward the hallway and started waving happily to someone nobody else could see.

PSI investigators visited the home in March 2003, and they had an interesting first meeting. Their digital camera kept fast forwarding. The images were not downloading and the dates and times on the video camera were malfunctioning. Equipment failure and malfunction are common in very haunted houses or places. Paranormal investigators everywhere are so used to cameras or flashlights losing power that they often bring several, just to be safe. PSI did a lengthy interview with the family and a thorough investigation of the property. They are now in the process of analyzing the data they collected and plan to do a follow-up investigation in the near future.

Though Jen is unsure about all of the history of their home, she does know that it was moved in the 1950s from its original location a few miles down the road to its current location, which was once farmland. She knows there was a large chicken farm in the backyard.

In fact, Scott had a vivid dream once about the chicken farm. An elderly gentleman who previously owned the home was giving him a tour of the property and specifically showed him where all of the chicken coops used to be.

This family is never alone. The house is never empty. And there is never a quiet moment, day or night. But they are accustomed to it and see no reason to change things. It's a fine example of how easily we can coexist with the spirit world, if we simply accept it and take it in stride.

Plattsburgh Air Force Base

Plattsburgh

There's no shortage of stories about the many haunted buildings on the old military base in Plattsburgh. In fact, I've received more e-mails about this particular haunted location than any other in the entire region. One man wrote, "I was stationed at Plattsburgh AFB from 1993-1995. While there, I heard of many unexplained events. For instance, I worked in the old headquarters building in front of the parade grounds. There were many nights I worked late and heard footsteps and doors opening and closing, even though nobody else was there. Some of my friends who worked in the two buildings to the left of mine had also heard weird things, like banging on the walls, screams, and footsteps. A lot of these people made sure they didn't have to work after hours, because they didn't want to be there after dark."

The Plattsburgh Air Force Base was a military base dating back to the Revolutionary War. The base closed in 1995, and today it is a sprawling—partially abandoned—industrial complex encompassing about 3,500 acres of land where private residences, offices, and commercial industries coexist. They are not the only things coexisting there. It seems there are a number of ghosts roaming the grounds among the living, according to those who have lived and worked there.

Many soldiers are buried in a cemetery on the old side of the base that's said to be haunted, some in unmarked graves from the "Battle of Plattsburgh." Children and infants were buried there early in the 1900s, as well. It's common knowledge that security police have seen apparitions of soldiers in both the cemetery and the adjacent crematorium, known as building #666—yes, really.

51

The basement of the military finance building was once a surgical ward for prisoners during the Revolutionary War. The walls are painted an ominous red, allegedly to conceal the bloodstains that were too difficult to wash out. People have heard screams coming from the basement where a fire was said to have burned many bed-ridden patients alive; even police K-9 units won't go down there.

Other buildings thought to be haunted are the old gymnasium, the base entrance, and an office. According to the rumor mill, the gym was at one time a morgue and, besides the proverbial screams in the night that are occasionally heard, staff at the gym say they've heard pounding coming from the doors where the morgue was. However, local historians can't confirm the validity of the morgue's location.

The entrance to the old base is also said to be haunted by a Revolutionary War soldier standing guard between the two original pillars. The surrounding woods are haunted, supposedly by the ghost of a woman dressed in white—or at least appearing to be dressed in white, which is the color of preference for ghosts! Ever notice how many times you hear a ghost story about "a woman in white?" That's because our limited human vision typically interprets spirit energy as a white, misty, or glowing apparition.

Those are the most common stories I've heard about the military base, but most of them are word of mouth and have been floating around for years, much like the ghosts they immortalize. They are well-known. But I wanted some first-hand accounts. Several people, like a retired aircraft mechanic who worked on the flight line, told me that the stories I'd heard about the base being haunted were true, because he had seen some "pretty weird stuff" himself.

Jimmy told me of a couple of "strange encounters" he'd had while working there. He said, "I used to work a lot of hours and would work on Saturday. Each of the staff took turns doing chores, and it was my turn to take out the garbage. I walked out the back door and down to the bin in the parking lot. When I turned around, I saw a man standing up against the building. I even thought I saw him smoking a cigarette. Expecting a new client that morning, I thought he had come by early, so I began jogging back to the office. I'm not the best judge of distance, but I'd be surprised if I was more than a few hundred feet away when I looked up at the door again and the man wasn't there. My worst fear was that the client entered the building without an escort—security was a main issue in this program. Upon entering the building . . . nothing. I searched every corner of the center. Nothing. I was puzzled but put it out of my mind."

Jimmy went on to describe the sounds he and his co-worker sometimes heard. "Once in a while, we would hear noises of footsteps coming down the front hallway when nobody was in the building but us. It was so apparent that we would open the closed door and peer down the hallway, expecting someone to be there. My co-worker even stopped coming in on Saturdays until I arrived. She didn't like the fact that the noises seemed so real, I guess. When I left that job, I met some folks who used to work on the base, and they confirmed that they knew of others who had heard noises, as well."

With the vast number of ghost stories I've heard related to the base—both word of mouth and first-hand accounts—I think it's safe to say that the base is one of our more haunted locations here in the North Country.

Soldier in Distress

Fort Drum

The area now designated as Fort Drum was known during World War II as Pine Camp. It was home to thousands of German and Italian prisoners of war between 1943 and 1946. Several of those prisoners—seven to be exact—died in 1944 and 1945 and are buried at Drum's Sheepfold Cemetery. The unmarked cemetery is rumored to be haunted, and it may well be; for this is where Dianne came upon the mysterious soldier.

In February 1993, Dianne was taking her son to a Cub Scout meeting on Fort Drum. The Boy Scout Hut is just off Route 26 before the bridge that goes into Great Bend. She saw the soldier standing by the side of the road on Route 26, waving his arm as if he was trying to flag her down. Because of the snow, she asked her young son and daughter if they saw him too, which they did—and as they got closer, he became very clear to all of them. Diane explained:

"He kept waving his arms until he realized I was slowing down. As I slowed down, he went back into the woods behind the cemetery. I could not see where he went, but I knew there were training spots back in that area. I figured someone got hurt and that the soldier went back to get whomever it was. So I waited.

"My husband is in the military, and I would want someone to help him if he was hurt. I waited and waited and waited. I stayed about twenty minutes, then I beeped my horn and called out, but there was no response. I didn't know what to do, so I decided to take my son to his meeting and then come back. I called out that I would be back and then left. I felt really bad about leaving, wondering if someone was hurt, but I left.

Photo by author

Seven POW gravestones at the Sheepfold Cemetery on Route 26, Fort Drum

"When I returned, I pulled over, got out of the car and called into the woods that I was back. I then returned to my car and stayed in the car with my daughter for another thirty minutes, but nobody ever came out of the woods. By then, it was time to go back and pick up my son. On my return home, as I came up to the cemetery, I again slowed down and looked for any sign that someone had come back. Finding nobody, I decided to go home. I still felt bad that I might have left someone in trouble, and it bothered me the whole night.

"The next day at work, I told the ladies what happened the night before, and one lady told me that Sheepfold Cemetery (sometimes called the POW Cemetery) is known to be haunted. She said it was the POWs whose graves sit off to the side of the civilian cemetery there. Since then, I've tried very hard to avoid passing that cemetery!"

If the ghost soldier—whether a POW or not—was seeking attention, he will finally start getting it at least once a year. Watertown's German-American Club held its first annual memorial for the POWs buried at Sheepfold on November 17, 2002. Perhaps, with this fitting recognition, the fallen POWs can finally find their way home—even though they were laid to rest on foreign ground.

The Streeter Homestead

North Gouverneur

Otis Streeter bought the Streeter Homestead from the Hartley estate around 1900. Streeters have owned and lived in the house since then. Diann Risley's grandfather, Glenn Streeter, bought the farm from Otis in 1915. When Glenn passed away in the early seventies, Diann moved into the home with her father and stepmother who continued to operate the family farm. It was then that she had her first—and, thankfully, only—encounter with the "pressure ghost."

Diann was sleeping upstairs in the old house she lived in with her father and stepmother when she was awakened by an unusual clicking noise. She had been listening to the strange sound for about ten minutes, trying to make sense of it, when a strong, invisible pressure was suddenly applied to her chest. Pressed firmly and helplessly against her mattress, she flailed her arms and legs, but to no avail. She tried to scream, but all that she managed was a guttural groan. It felt as if someone had their hand over her mouth and was trying to smother her. *It felt as if someone was forcing CPR on her while she was awake and alert.* When she finally found her voice and yelled out, the unseen weight lifted and the menacing presence abruptly disappeared. Except for her throbbing heartbeat reverberating in her eardrums, all was quiet once again, but Diann spent the rest of the night sitting up uneasily in a chair "on guard."

Twenty years later in the early nineties, Diann was back at her childhood home, known as the Streeter Homestead. It is located a few miles north of the village of Gouverneur on the Rock Island Road. She and her son, Jason, were staying at the farm—which has been in the Streeter family for more than a century—while they moved from one home to another. The boy was very sick with the flu, so when someone appeared at the door to Diann's bedroom in the middle of the night, she thought they were getting her to go to her son. She could see a figure of a woman, holding a white bundle close to her chest. As Diann's eyes adjusted to the darkness, the figure became clearer. Diann lay motionless, stunned as the figure walked toward her, straight through her bed, and out the wall on the other side.

Diann believes the female ghost passing through her bedroom that night may be a young mother named Mary, who was laid to rest in the North Gouverneur Cemetery in 1890, after she and her infant son succumbed to cholera. Perhaps it was the smell of sickness in her former home that drew the woman and her son back that evening. Diann had found out about Mary while in high school in the sixties. She did a gravestone rubbing for the Yorkers Club and came upon the stones of Mary and her son in a cemetery adjacent to the massive 232-acre farm "out behind the barn toward the old orchard." The memory of Mary had all but faded until the night Diann woke to find the restless woman wandering through the house. Could the white bundle the ghost cradled against her bosom that night be the tiny child she was buried beside?

Two of her cousins were playing records in the front upstairs bedroom one day when an apparition of a man came toward them. It's hard to say who disappeared faster—the girls, who ran off screaming, or the ghost! Years later, Diann's daughter saw a hand reach over and pull back the curtains in that very same bedroom. Diann had told her to wait in the car while she ran a prescription in to her father, who was alone at the time. When she returned to the car, her daughter asked Diann who the man was in that upstairs bedroom. Diann was stumped. Her father had been the only one home, and she knew he wasn't in that room.

Diann's aunt often spoke of a loud knock on the landing door, but whenever anyone went to answer it, nobody was there. They became so accustomed to it that they would jokingly say, "It's only the ghost again." While Diann lived in the home, her father and stepmother constantly complained of losing things and of lights being turned on when nobody was there. Diann has sensed for a long time that there were others present at the homestead; others who weren't often seen. She gets a tight, uncomfortable feeling—as if she is intruding on someone—in many of the rooms in the large house and especially in the horse barn. Though she hasn't heard of any particular events occurring in the barn, she feels something must have, because the most disturbing feelings she gets are in the barn and the woodshed. Unfortunately, since her father passed away, there are not many people left who could shed some light on the past circumstances of the outbuildings.

Diann's nephew and his family currently live in the home, and they have not experienced anything out of the ordinary. Perhaps the ghosts have finally moved on.

With such a long history and so many people having lived there, it's hard to know who was haunting the Streeter Homestead. But there seemed to be a number of ghosts of differing personalities— some good, some not.

The Boice Homestead

Lisbon

The vacant Boice Homestead, Route 37, Lisbon

Many people have driven past the abandoned Boice Homestead on Route 37 in Lisbon and claimed to have seen the face of a boy in an upstairs window. That is one reason why the old home is believed to be haunted. Nobody knows who the boy might be, so his story can't be told. However, there is a story that can be told of a woman who killed herself in the home and subsequently frightened more than one visitor away. Her name was Myrtle Putney.

Myrtle Putney was a 22-year-old Lisbon school teacher who shot herself in the heart at the home of her aunt, Mrs. E.J. Boice, during Independence Day fireworks on July 4, 1917. According to newspaper accounts, the young woman had been depressed and in ill health. A newspaper article titled "Miss Myrtle Putney Commits Suicide" in the *Ogdensburg Advance* and *St. Lawrence Weekly Democrat* on July 5, 1917, said:

> The village of Lisbon was greatly aroused last evening when it became known that Miss Myrtle Putney, 22, daughter of Mr. and Mrs. John Putney, had taken her life shortly after seven o'clock…while suffering from a fit of despondency.
>
> Miss Putney had been about the house with other members of the family during the early part of the evening. About seven o'clock, she complained of feeling tired and retired to her room to lie down and rest.
>
> A few minutes afterward, the family was startled by the report of a pistol shot. Her sister immediately investigated and was horrified to find the young woman lying on the floor dead with a .38 caliber bullet in her body.

A week later, the *Ogdensburg Advance* and *St. Lawrence Weekly Democrat* reported that, "Miss Putney was despondent over ill health which was responsible for committing the rash act." It continued:

> As a result of the coroner's investigation in the matter of the death of Miss Myrtle Putney, the 22-year-old Lisbon school teacher who shot herself last week, it developed that the young woman had been suffering from poor health for some time. At times she was very despondent, but of late there was considerable of an improvement, and it was thought that the period of depression had passed.
>
> The funeral was held Friday from the house, Rev. Mr. Hill of the Wesleyan Methodist Church officiating, and interment was made in Sucker Brook cemetery, Lisbon.

There are many theories as to why she may have taken her life. Ray Kentner, a 104-year-old Lisbon resident who was at the home that evening, said there were rumors that Ms. Putney was "pining over someone," but nobody ever knew her to be seeing anyone. He went on to say, unabashedly as someone of his years is entitled to, that the shooting "kind of put a damper on the rest of the day's events."

Some have suggested—in an attempt to explain the young woman's mysterious ill health and despair leading up to the event—

that she might have been "with child" and jilted by her lover. Finally, a few have even speculated that perhaps she was murdered; however, all indications at the time pointed to suicide, and no further evidence to the contrary has ever been presented. Any of those theories might explain why Myrtle was unable to rest in peace for so many years after her passing. Maybe there was something more that she wanted everyone—or *any*one—to understand about the events that unfolded the night of her death.

Lisbon resident, Diane Gusa, rented the old Boice Homestead from 1976 to 1978. It's in an area of Lisbon called "Putneyville," because so many people along that stretch of highway are related, I was told. She recalled that every night she heard voices around ten or eleven, and every night her husband told her it was just the wind in the pipes. She knew what she heard, though, and on one particularly quiet night, she heard a woman talking. She couldn't make out the words, but she could hear the inflections in the woman's voice. It sounded as if the mysterious woman was having an animated conversation with someone, but nobody else's voice was heard. Again, Diane woke her husband, and again, he said, "no" to the idea that there was anyone talking besides he and his wife.

The following month, Diane and her husband had friends visit them from Australia. Even though the upstairs was not to be used by the tenants, Diane used a skeleton key to enter through a locked door and was delighted to find the rooms all furnished with "antiques and other beautiful things." She cleaned one of the upstairs rooms for their guests—an old room in the back right corner of the home. The first night that the couple from Australia were there, the wife decided to retire to her room early. The others were sitting around chatting downstairs, when they heard a blood-curdling scream from the woman. As the woman's husband flew out of his chair and up the stairs, Diane noted that it was ten or eleven p.m.—about the same time she had become accustomed to hearing a woman's voice each night.

The husband returned about forty-five minutes later and said, "I can't leave my wife for long. I'll see you in the morning." The next morning when the couple came downstairs, Diane asked them what happened. The husband said, "Well, you know we don't have two-story houses in Australia, and there are trees, so maybe she got into a Hitchcock moment. But she saw something, and she doesn't think we should tell you what she saw, because you wouldn't want to live here." Diane didn't press for more details. She already had formed her own suspicions anyway.

Not long after the incident with the Australian guests, a neighbor came by to visit. Diane blurted out, "Eileen, is this house haunted?" The reply was, "Oh, yeah. Don't you know about Myrtle?" Diane later found out that Myrtle died in the same room she had prepared for their Australian guests.

Diane didn't have a problem with Myrtle being there, because she certainly wasn't a malicious spirit. But her sister-in-law didn't appreciate her meddling presence. Diane had her whole family up for Thanksgiving, and they were all using the upstairs rooms. Her sister-in-law went to bed early, and around 10:30 or 11 p.m., she came down to the living room where the rest of the family was gathered and demanded to know who woke her up. She was quite upset, and, with her hands on her hips in a "don't-mess-with-me" pose, she insisted that someone had just been in her room and said, "Miss, Miss, wake up." Interestingly, the sister-in-law's name was Missy. Diane was half kidding when she said, "Well, it couldn't have been any of us. We call you Missy, not Miss. It must've been the ghost." At that moment, Missy realized that she had seen *through* the figure that appeared in her room and woke her up. It hadn't registered until Diane mentioned the word 'ghost.'

In May of 1978, Diane awoke one morning to find all of the many doors in the house wide open. There was no explanation for it, but Diane has an interesting theory. She feels that the 22-year-old Myrtle died prematurely in 1917. If the young woman would have gone on to live a full life, she could have expected to live until 1978 or so—when she would have been 83. Maybe her time on the earthly plane had finally come to its natural conclusion that morning, and she let Diane know she was leaving by opening all of the doors.

Sandy Putney learned all about Myrtle when she married into the Putney family. The family so strongly believes that Myrtle was (or is) still there, that they find themselves saying, "Hi, Myrtle!" whenever they drive by the house. Sandy has personally heard Myrtle crying in the upstairs bedrooms three times, when her friend, Diane Gusa, lived there. "It was a heartbroken sobbing, and you could tell it was coming from upstairs," she said.

In the summer of 2002, a man doing renovation work on the Boice house quit because of happenings he believed were caused by Myrtle—or some other ghost in residence. He didn't even go back to get his equipment, which had not been working anyway—thanks to the ghost or ghosts. He claimed that his tools were shorting out for no apparent reason. He found his truck tires flat, and the truck wouldn't start. He felt the presence of someone there so strongly, in fact, that he refused to ever go back.

The house is still known locally as the "Boice House" and is undergoing renovation. The property is private and should not be trespassed on, but you may see a ghostly face in the window as you drive by.

The Hall Residence

Theresa

Photo by author

The Hall Residence at 216 High Street, Theresa

If you live with something bizarre long enough, it becomes normal to you. And when it becomes normal, you lose the fear you originally had of it. When Robin Hall got flipped out of bed one morning by unseen hands, she wasn't afraid. She was annoyed. She climbed grumpily back into bed, cussed, yanked the covers up over herself, and told whatever it was to leave her alone so she could sleep. Enough was enough.

Jeff Hall, Robin's husband, has lived in the home at 216 High Street for several years now. It's a two-story house with a barn and an old milk-factory-turned-oil-plant beside it. A nearby cemetery on a hill across the road looks down on their house. When Jeff first purchased the property, he brought a mirror with him that had been in a house where a triple murder occurred many years ago. That may have been a mistake. The mirror is being stored in their barn for now. Since then, a lot of strange things have happened in that barn. Robin quips, "Mirror, mirror on the wall, send the ghosts to Jeffrey Hall."

Robin's ten-year-old son had objects repeatedly fall in the barn as he walked past them, while Robin and Jeff watched in disbelief. The boy lives with his biological father out of state, but he comes up north for visits occasionally. He has seen a very bright light and the appearance of a figure at the end of his bed. While paranormal activity occurs when he is not present, it seems to increase when he is there. Sounds of movement and footsteps have been heard across the upper level of the barn, and the family feels like they are always being watched in the building. No wonder. Shadows have been seen moving throughout the barn, especially when someone is searching for intruders. Now Robin's son refuses to go into the barn alone.

The barn, however, is not the only building affected by paranormal activity on the property. The main house sees plenty of action, and that's where it really gets physical. The couple's bed has shaken

Photo by author

The barn adjacent to the Hall Residence

them awake, and Jeff would rather not sleep upstairs because he gets "grabbed" at night—no, not by his wife—nor anyone else they can see, for that matter. Jeff's not as feisty as Robin is when it comes to dealing with the ghost. Besides being thrown out of her own bed that one time, Robin said she has also felt the bed "bow" beneath her, even when she was wide awake. And when only one of them is in the bed, they sometimes feel someone else sit or lie down beside them. But even stranger yet, Jeff once heard the sound of a female's snore emanating from the bed when he was alone. That's something I haven't heard in a ghost story before! He even got up and walked around the bed trying to determine the source of the sound, but it remains a mystery. No wonder Robin cursed the presence for throwing her out of bed. It's a miracle the couple gets any sleep at all.

Throughout the rest of the house, dark shadows and orbs have been seen moving, lights flick on and off, and doors open and close, sometimes with great force. Objects are moved from one spot to another, like the time Robin had laid out fresh towels as she hopped into the shower, only to find them upstairs on her bed when she came out. And, of course, there is "the cold spot." Every haunted house seems to have one. Although the house is very well-insulated with no discernible drafts, there is a definite cold spot at the top of the stairs where Robin and Jeff have seen a shadow passing from room to room. There are no windows or power outlets in that location, and as soon as you pass beyond the spot, the air returns to the usual temperature again.

On Halloween night in 2002, Robin made herself a bowl of soup for dinner and sat on the couch waiting for trick-or-treaters. Jeff was out of town working, and the children were in Florida. Just seconds before the first knock on the door, a witch decoration fell from on top of a cupboard to the floor. At the door were two little witches. Robin got the trick and the girls got their treats!

At the end of May 2003, Robin had a bizarre dream—or something. Jeff had left early to work out of town, and Robin had fallen asleep. Before she woke, she said she "was a participant in a strange happening." Someone or something grabbed her by the nape of the neck and dragged her one or two feet at a time, from Jeff's side of the bed to her side. At the same time, a vision of Jeff appeared at the top of the stairs between the bedroom doors. Robin doesn't know if it was some type of out-of-body experience or a sign from their occasional visitors. The rest of the day, Robin was out of sorts. She said she "felt spacey, like something was missing," and, before anyone could beat her to the punch, she joked that it was not because she's a blonde! At the end of the day, Jeff came home and asked her what was wrong. He told her she looked pale, and she told him she had looked that way all day. Then she told him of the latest incident.

PSI investigated the home and took a detailed history of events. They also made recordings to analyze for electronic voice phenomenon (EVP) and took dozens of photographs. They noted in their report that they were able to detect a definite cold spot in the stairway and could find no usual explanation for that abnormality. They said that "analysis of EVP recordings totaling about sixteen hours of tape and digital recordings from several machines resulted in a possible three-second recording of what might appear to be the sound of a woman's laughter, but the example was faint and shrouded." Though nothing else conclusive turned up on film or tape during their first visit, that's not to say that there isn't something going on there. If only it were that easy to capture hard evidence of spirit activity when you're well equipped, prepared, and waiting.

Perhaps it was merely a day of rest for the living *and* the dead in the Hall home the day the investigators arrived . . . and sleep is something they could sure use.

The Hand House

Elizabethtown

Photo by author

The Hand House, Elizabethtown

I've heard ghost stories from all kinds of people—businessmen, politicians, medical personnel, teachers, farmers, homemakers, and so on—but I've never heard of a ghost encounter that happened to a Franciscan friar, until now.

The elegant Hand House on River Street has been owned and maintained since 1978 by the Bruce L. Crary Foundation—a not-for-profit organization dedicated to providing educational opportunities for students in the area by handing out 500 scholarships a year. Hannelore "Hanna" Kissam is the Executive Director of the Foundation; and, as such, she enjoys more time in the home than anyone else. But the building is open to the public for community meetings throughout the year, by appointment. Although it's not the norm, visitors are occasionally permitted to sleep there for various legitimate reasons; after all, there are plenty of bedrooms.

The beautiful old home, built by illustrious North Country lawyer, Augustus C. Hand in 1849, has at least five bedrooms that were used by his family and hired help. Each bedroom has been restored to closely resemble its original appearance, and many of the genuine possessions of the Hand family can be found throughout.

Six years ago, Hanna's son was ordained as a Franciscan friar at an ordination ceremony in Westport. The Hand House was used to assist with lodging for the overflow of attendees at the ceremony, so Hanna's son and a fellow friar shared one of the bedrooms. The room the two young men shared faces the street and has twin beds. It's quite attractive and comfortable.

Sometime during the night, the other friar was awakened by the sound of footsteps coming down the hall toward the room he was in. He then saw, by the light of a passing automobile, the door slowly opening, but there was nobody there. He was already paralyzed by fear when he felt something sit, and then *lie*, down on his bed—right on top of him! After perhaps ten minutes had gone by—minutes that must have seemed like an eternity to the poor man of the cloth—he felt the weight of the spectral body lift and heard the footsteps going back toward the door. As he yanked the blankets up over his head, he heard the door open and close and then listened as the footsteps faded, continuing back down the hall from which they came.

At the first sign of daybreak, the shaken young cleric promptly left the premises, never to sleep there again. Hanna's son slept soundly through the entire incident and never noticed a thing. But Hanna was not at all alarmed by the other friar's experience. She has spent many days and nights in the Hand House, and she has grown very fond of the place. However, she has had her share of unexplained incidents in the home. She once spent six weeks straight convalescing in a lovely bedroom on the second floor following surgery. Besides often seeing shadows out of the corner of her eye, she has heard doorknobs turn and footsteps outside of her bedroom door. One night she bravely got up to see who it was, but all she saw was a "vaporous, misty, smoky figure going through the door of the servants' quarters," which was just down the hall from her bedroom.

Photo by author

Second-floor hallway as seen from bedroom Hanna recovered in. The old servant's quarters is on right beyond the stairway railing.

Summer interns rooming in the servants' quarters have left and refused to come back to the house, according to Hanna. And an artist/illustrator who stayed in the home while illustrating a regional book admitted to seeing something unexplained several times.

Hanna feels the ghost is of a young woman, because the odor that accompanies the vaporous mist and passing chill is "like that of a woman who hasn't bathed in a while," which was the norm a hundred years ago. There's also a very faint smell of perfume, "an invisible cloud of it," she says, that Hanna sometimes walks through. She always feels a chill when that happens. Who could the woman be? Hanna doesn't dare speculate. Too many people have passed through the exquisite home in the last 150 years to even hazard a guess. But the atmosphere of Hand House is so regal, peaceful, and appealing that any one of the people who have passed through it might be fond enough of the home to want to stay there indefinitely.

The Harison-Morley Grist Mill

Morley

Photo by author

Harison-Morley Grist Mill, Morley

It was broad daylight on a nice, sunny day when Charlie saw Jeff, the carpenter, running up the road toward him. He was as white as a ghost and all bug-eyed. Charlie knew something must be wrong, because Jeff would never leave his tools unattended at the worksite unless there was a real emergency. Why, he loved those tools as much as his own kids! Jeff breathlessly told Charlie he'd better come quickly. Something strange was going on down at the grist mill.

As the two men entered the mill, Jeff explained that he had heard someone walking back and forth overhead on the second floor—a wide open space at that time. He was the only person at the mill and hadn't seen anyone come in, but there was no doubt in his mind that he heard footsteps. Charlie teased his friend that he was probably "drunker than a skunk!" But they both knew that wasn't true. Someone must have come in when Jeff wasn't looking and was snooping around up there, Charlie figured.

Just then, the footsteps started back up, and both men heard them at the same time. Now, certain that they had an intruder, Charlie dashed up the stairs to the second floor, but it was empty. Then he sprinted up to the third floor, sure that he was hot on the heels of the prowler. Again, nothing. Nobody was in the building, except Charlie and Jeff. Realizing this, Charlie bolted down the stairs; and at the same time, a curious Jeff was cautiously starting up them, hopeful that Charlie had found a logical explanation for the footsteps. However, the moment Jeff looked at Charlie's face, he knew it wasn't good. For the second time that day, he spun around and raced out of the building.

As word of the haunted grist mill quickly spread, Charlie sought the opinions of paranormal investigators. One team of investigators from the Central New York area captured film footage of several orbs coming up off from the floor before vanishing. They also heard the sound of something dragging across the floor upstairs, which is why Jeff—now fully recovered from the shock of his initial encounter with the unknown intruder—fondly refers to the specter as "Igor." "Igor's at it again," he'll say. Charlie believes that whoever is haunting the mill is simply interested in seeing its restoration, a common reason for visitations from the other side. He said he feels nothing but peacefulness in the building now.

Charlie LaShombe is the executive director of the Heritage Grist Mill Association, a non-profit organization dedicated to restoring the 160-year-old Harison-Morley Grist Mill to provide students and tourists with "a living museum," where they can experience an authentic, old-time working mill, just as it was in its heyday. Because of the educational and historical value of such a project, the volunteer association receives funding through grants and private and corporate donations.

The Haunted Postcard

Rossie

"Every time there's history, there are ghost stories—there are murders. We have very famous murders here. This man that walks without a head..."

Sandy Wyman – Town of Rossie Historian

Long ago a man was decapitated at the Baken Inn which once sat at the corner of the old Lead Mine and River Roads. It happened before the Civil War, so there are no records indicating who he was or why he was beheaded. He may have been a transient pack peddler who came to town with a pack of goods to sell to the people working in the mines. Many pack peddlers back then came up missing, killed for what little goods they had. Stories of local murders and missing people were commonplace in those days. Although he wasn't the only man murdered at the hotel, he is mentioned in this book, because his distinctive apparition remained at the Inn for some time after his death. And wherever his ghost drifted about, the ghoulish shriek of a woman was almost always heard. It was described as sounding like the scream of an angry bobcat about to attack, and it was every bit as blood-curdling.

Another famous murder in the Town of Rossie was that of Jimmy Todd, and it happened in a room at the old Rossie Hotel. His ghost was said to haunt the hotel until it burned in 1986. He must have had a lot of company, because a previous owner admitted that he heard footsteps in the hotel all the time. He would be sitting in the living room alone at night, after business hours, and clearly hear people coming and going, walking up and down the stairs, and opening and closing the hotel's many doors. It sounded like a bustling hotel—the way it was during its heyday—yet nobody else was around.

There are many other ghost stories in the Rossie area, according to current Town of Rossie Historian, Sandra Wyman, a woman of great wit and spunk. She has collected local historical memorabilia all her life and shared her vast knowledge of Rossie's mysterious happenings with me. There's the old stone house that once stood in Oxbow. They couldn't keep the doors shut. Ghosts would walk in the door, through the house, up the stairs, back downstairs, and back out the door. Many people saw and heard these things.

There's also a house that was destined to continue burning in Hammond. Every time they built a house in that spot, it would burn to the ground. They'd build it, it would burn. They'd build another house, and it, too, would burn. No loss of life is known about, but when the original structure burned down, whoever owned it didn't want anyone else taking its place.

Then there were the Helmer girls, who heard a very loud horse and buggy coming at them on the dirt road in front of the Helmer House and Hotel, so they quickly jumped out of the way, but they never saw anything pass by. That happened sometime between the Civil War and 1876, and the story was so compelling that it is forever a part of Rossie's colorful history.

After admitting to me, "I'm skeptical enough not to believe in everything, but not stupid enough to believe that there's nothing out there," Ms. Wyman told me of her father's personal experience while growing up in Brasie Corners. Before World War I, he had told her, there was a man who walked every day from his house on Route 58 to Pope Mills where he would go to the store or local tavern, and at nightfall, he would walk back home, carrying his lantern. One day when Ms. Wyman's father and his family went by the man's house, they found it had burnt to the ground, with the man in it. For many, many years—until the new road was constructed in 1978—people saw a lantern going down the road, just a lantern—traveling by itself in mid-air. Ms. Wyman's father even saw it. Too many local folks saw it, in fact, to ignore it. The old man with the lantern apparently continued returning home nightly, long after his death.

Many of the town's ghost stories are memorialized in the "Rossie Tour Poem," written for past Rossie historian, Vergie Simons, in 1951 by Kate Petrie. Ms. Wyman said the two women did much to preserve the history of Rossie.

Rossie Tour Poem

At Dupontville we turned and went over sand hill
Here we heard a story which gave us a chill
As we passed the site of the old Baken Inn
A famous night spot where they shouldn't sell gin
But as sometimes is done, they sold just the same
And the authorities made short of their little old game
Now this same hotel, because it was small
Became known as the Tiddle de Wink and the Hole in the Wall

Here murders were committed and stories have been told
As they've been handed down by generations of old
About a headless man walking as if on a stair
While the screams of a woman pierced the night air
Along the Oswegatchie River we rode with delight
Past a haunted house ruins, where doors never shut tight
On toward Wegatchie which was once Church Mills
Where another haunted house gave people chills

Passing over a knoll, the guides told of a fright
Which happened to two girls one very dark night
They heard horses' hooves running, so fast did they come
That the buggy wheels turning made a very loud hum
So the two girls quickly moved out of the way
To let the vehicle pass without any delay
But nothing ever passed by that they could see
What they heard that night is still a mystery

As we moved along, the guides on the tour
Pointed out the Rossie Hotel, the same as of yore
Built in 1811 by a land holder, David Parish
There's a story to tell, which old people cherish
About Jimmie Todd, who was there most of all
He was killed and months later found in Tammany Hall

If hearing old ghost stories of yesteryear doesn't particularly spook you like you want to be spooked, take a look at the following postcard Ms. Wyman recently acquired. It's titled, "Bird's Eye View of Rossie, N.Y.," and it's supposed to simply be a photograph of the town, but an apparition in front of one of the buildings to the left and center of the postcard looks like a man smiling at the camera. The one-cent postage stamp used on the back of the postcard was issued in 1903, so that dates the photograph to the late nineteenth century or the very first years of the twentieth century. We've not seen another like it and have no clue as to its history. But we do know one thing for certain; it isn't the ghost of the headless man!

Courtesy of S. Wyman

Postcard from 1903, with mysterious apparition of a smiling man in front of the buildings to the left and center of the photograph

The House on the Hill

Westville

"Oh, that's Sharon in her knee-length, fluffy nightgown," Jean thought groggily, as she watched something white gliding past the foot of their bed toward her bureau one night. Then she remembered that her daughter Sharon was spending the night at a friend's house. She frantically woke her late husband, Arthur, and told him there was someone in their room—someone who looked perhaps like a boy with his shirttail hanging out. He thought she was crazy at the time—he would change his mind soon enough.

The house sits on top of a hill on the Westville Trout River Road, Route 20, in Westville. An early settler to the Westville area built the original home on the property, but it was destroyed by fire, and the home Jean and Arthur owned was built in its place.

Jean's first ghostly encounter in the home, described above, happened about ten years after they moved in. It was followed by a string of encounters and unexplained events that spanned several decades and involved every member of the family, as well as family friends.

Besides seeing the "white gliding" figure, Jean also turned on her side one night to find a misty grayish form of a man standing there beside her bed. She recalls, "He had a high waist. I remember the pant legs, a belt around the waist, a part of the shirt tucked in at the waist. Either there was nothing else, or I did not take time to look because I ducked under the covers so quickly."

Arthur told Jean that, in 1963, while she was in England, having been summoned overseas due to the illness of her father, he knew before she even called that her father had died. He explained how he saw a ball of light during the night that was hovering on the window ledge, and he felt that it was the spirit of his father-in-law. Another incident occurred while Jean was in England. Arthur was mowing the grass at the Brigg Street Cemetery when he felt someone run a finger down his spine. He said it felt as though he was "caught on a bramble bush," but he was in the middle of the cemetery where there was nothing nearby that could have touched him on his back.

The couple kept their mysterious experiences to themselves, and after Arthur passed away, Jean sold the house to Sharon and her husband and moved next door.

Sharon recalls hearing footsteps when nobody was there and said that her son Derek saw what looked like "a man in the corner wearing small glasses who was looking at him" on a couple of occasions. Not surprisingly, he fled from his upstairs bedroom and refused to go back to sleep that night. Sharon's friend who was sleeping over one night woke to see a misty cloud float to the ceiling and disappear. She declined any future invitations to spend the night there. Is it any wonder why?

The Missing Tombstone

Cape Vincent

In her last will and testament, a Cape Vincent woman stated that, upon her death and that of all remaining family and kin, their gravestones be clearly marked with their names and dates of birth and death. As directed, the family's gravestones were clustered together in the St. Lawrence Cemetery on County Road 4 in Cape Vincent. They're all still there—all marked accordingly—all except the woman's own gravestone. That's the only one missing, which is a bit odd, since she was the one who left the original instructions more than a hundred years ago. Maybe she took it with her when she rose from her grave, assuming that it's her ghost that's been haunting her former home lately.

The man who built the old farmhouse in Cape Vincent in 1842 died in 1854. His widow—the one whose gravestone came up missing—and their children managed to keep the farm running until the 1880s, when the property was passed on to their son and his grandsons who kept it in the family until the 1930s. Finally, the farmhouse was sold to someone outside of the family. The current owner, John, bought the old home in 1999 and moved his family of five "up north" from Niagara County.

The problems started almost immediately upon closing on their new 157-year-old home. The water and electric were in obvious need of repair. The foundation, at first glance, would also need some minor repair. Luckily, John is very handy and can fix almost anything. However, a closer inspection of the foundation, after work on the home had commenced, revealed major structural damage to the foundation on one side of the home. If John had been aware of that information prior to closing on the property, he never would have purchased the home. And there were other problems, as well—problems that even the handiest handyman could never repair.

John's wife was working the third shift as a registered nurse when they moved into the home, so John spent the first few nights asleep on the living room floor, alone, until their upstairs bedroom was ready. One of those nights, he was awakened when he felt a "huge pressure" on his head, "as if someone was standing on it or sitting on it." He could not move his head at all, and the pressure got heavier and heavier. He knew his dog was lying next to him, so he reached his arm out to touch her, and the pressure disappeared.

Another night, John was again alone in the living room, mulling over what he should do about the house and the deplorable condition of the foundation. All of a sudden, a string of lights of different colors appeared in front of him and floated across the living room, moving up and down, as they made their way out into the dining room. John called his wife at work and told her what he saw—and that he had suddenly decided that he would fix the house.

During reconstruction of the foundation and remodeling of the living room, John witnessed "several visions." One was an elderly man with a long white beard, whose image manifested in the front window of the living room. Another was an elderly woman wearing a bonnet. They both seemed to be standing on the front porch looking *into* the living room, as John sat there looking out at them. They must have been curious about what was being done to their old home. Needless to say, as soon as the master bedroom was ready upstairs, John would never again sleep in the living room, which had been the center of paranormal activity since they moved in. But there was also activity in other parts of the home. For example, John once watched what appeared to be a man dressed in black walk out of another room in the home and disappear. He has also experienced mysterious happenings in the basement and the barn.

Getting the house up to code and livable was a massive undertaking for the new homeowner, and he found himself always busy doing plumbing, electrical, and so on. It was during this time that his tools started coming up missing. One time he was working in the basement and had just set down two tools, but when he turned around to get them, they were gone. His tools were disappearing and reappearing at an alarming rate during renovations, and he'd had enough of it. He called to his son and daughter to come down and help him find them. Finally, the tools were discovered in a different part of the house, hidden underneath some paper!

As in many old barns, the timber in John's barn was covered with names and signatures of previous owners and their hired help. One day while John and his son were removing some of the long planks so they could use them for other things, a plank that was nailed in suddenly slammed down on John's fingers. Gripped by severe pain, he fumbled with his free hand to grab a nearby crowbar and pried his fingers loose. He saw some writing on the plank but couldn't make it out in the dim light. Getting more light on the subject, he discovered the name of the original owner from the 1880s painted on it. He decided he didn't need to use the plank just yet, after all.

The home no longer seems haunted, so John speculates that the spirits must be happy with how he has taken care of the house. It is often noted that paranormal activity begins when remodeling begins and ends when remodeling ends; and that certainly seems to the be case here.

The Old Man

North Lawrence

"It began with what seemed like a nightmare, but now I believe it was an attempt by a departed old man to welcome me to his home," said Faith. She and her husband Jerry live on County Route 55 in North Lawrence in a home built in 1864, a home the locals refer to as "the house where that man hung himself in the barn." Understandably, it is the talk of the town quite often. At one time it was because of the puzzling nature of the hanging, but now it's because of the well-known, unexplainable incidents that have occurred there since the hanging.

Almost immediately strange things began to happen when Faith moved into her husband's house seven years ago. On one of her first nights there, she had a dream that an elderly man was standing at the head of their bed with his hands "resting gently" on her shoulders while looking down at her. She says, "When I awoke, I felt around to find where my husband's hands were placed, only to find that he was positioned in the opposite direction. I woke him and he assured me that I'd just had a bad dream. Nevertheless, the TV and bedside lamp remained on throughout the rest of the night."

Faith soon learned that a man had hung himself from a rafter in the barn behind the house in a tragic event shrouded in mystery. Several neighbors and the local barber who saw the man on the day he chose to die said he was acting no differently than usual that morning. He went to the barber shop and got his hair cut and was paid a visit by a neighbor—a daily routine—sharing in conversation and discussing local news over coffee. The neighbor noted that there was nothing out of the ordinary. Later that day, as an elderly female neighbor returned a wheelbarrow she had borrowed to the old man's barn, she found him hanging. As is oftentimes the case, nobody knows why he did what he did. But maybe he's been having second thoughts.

Jerry's sister told Faith of a slumber party at the house years before Faith moved in during which several guests saw "an old man sitting at the top of the stairs." That same night, the girls all went outside, and one of the girls spotted an old man sitting on the couch through the living room window. Needless to say, nobody wanted to go upstairs or *anywhere* alone the rest of the evening. There was also an upstairs telephone that rang, when no other phones in the house were ringing, and when someone answered it, they only heard a dial tone.

Faith recalls many incidents that have occurred since her "welcoming nightmare." She tells of a time when Jerry brought her father upstairs to see the progress of renovations on the second floor. Her stepson, just a toddler at the time, followed them up but returned back downstairs moments later screaming that he had "seen the man" in the bedroom. It was not the same room Jerry or Faith's father had been in. Their youngest son also told Faith one day, as she got him dressed to go somewhere, that there was a man sitting on their couch. Considering everything else she had already experienced and heard about, she knew he wasn't kidding. "I've never dressed him faster!" she exclaimed.

Lights and fixtures seem to be pretty popular targets for ghosts and spirits to manipulate, and that has certainly been the case at this home. One night Jerry and Faith returned home to find the light on a porch they never use had been turned on. Nobody was at their house while they were away that they knew of. Another time, the lights went out while the couple was hanging a wallpaper border in their son's newly-remodeled bedroom. Neither was anywhere near the switch at the time.

The bathroom faucet was tampered with on another occasion. Faith watched her youngest son go into the bathroom to wash off a toy truck he had brought inside. She had a clear view of the bathroom and her son from where she sat at her computer desk. She recalls that shortly after he left the bathroom, the faucet turned itself back on "full throttle."

The Little Tykes kitchen play set sits in the corner of the living room. In order to activate the many kitchen sounds, you have to turn a knob. Faith said that every once in awhile, the sounds come on by themselves, and she and the boys joke that it must be the ghost.

The ghost also likes to hide things, like ghosts often do. The family's contractor keeps a close eye on his equipment, so when his sawsall blade came up missing when he returned to work one day, he immediately noticed and asked where it was. He had set it right on the windowsill of the room he was working in, but it was gone. Everyone searched the area thoroughly, but they couldn't find it. Faith explained to him, half teasingly, that it was probably their ghost and it would turn up exactly where he said he'd left it. Sure enough, the next day, it was in plain view right on the windowsill. They all had a good laugh about it.

Last summer during a barbecue, Faith brought a friend in to see some old black and white photographs her grandmother had given her. She knew she had placed them in the desk. The women searched and searched, however, and they couldn't find them. Just then, they heard the friend's husband arrive, so they left the room for a moment to greet him. When the three of them returned to the room to find the photographs, Faith said, "Unbelievably, there they sat in plain sight on the desk my friend and I had just searched! My friend stood in disbelief and explained to her husband we had searched the desk moments ago. Their child, my children, and my husband had remained outside during the whole episode. Mysterious!"

One night when Faith was trying to find some information on the internet about her house and the man who hung himself, she became frustrated at her lack of luck. Shoving herself away from the computer desk, she grabbed a magazine to get her mind off the man for a moment. Just as she was flipping through the magazine, the keyboard started slowly rolling out from under the desk where she had pushed it in. She thought nothing of it, figuring it was the cats, because nobody was near the computer; and she pushed it back in. A few moments later, she noticed the cats playing across the room, and at the same moment, a little more forcefully, the keyboard came rolling out again. That time, Faith immediately thought of the ghost and said aloud that she was done looking for information about him for the day. It hasn't happened since. In fact, it had never happened before the night she was researching the man, and it hasn't happened since she told him she was finished.

Even though she believes their ghost is pleasant and harmless, as most are, Faith admits he can be mischievous. In her words, "Our friend seems to have the most fun with my youngest son. One night when he was just a toddler, he ran a high fever. I got the Motrin out of the refrigerator, noted the time (4:00 a.m.), and told my husband the medicine was in the fridge and when the next dose was to be given. When we woke up, the Motrin was nowhere to be found. I told my husband that if we bought another bottle at the local store, we'd probably return to find the missing bottle. Sure enough, after returning home, the original bottle was found in the door of the fridge, right where I had placed it at 4:00 a.m.!"

"On another occasion, we had purchased a Scooby Doo Christmas ornament, and my son carried it with him everywhere. He wanted to take a bath, so he put the ornament on the seat of the recliner next to the couch his father was lying on. After his bath, we searched and searched for the ornament with no success. About a week later, my husband said, 'I found the ornament!' As he lay on the couch, he spotted a lump directly under the throw rug that's in the middle of the living room—a rug we walk across daily!"

Increasingly curious about the possibility of living in a haunted house, Faith visited a psychic who described the hallway and stairwell in her home accurately, even adding correctly that the area was the coldest in the house. She told Faith their spirit was a man who stayed mostly in that area and offered his initials, which Faith later confirmed matched the initials of the man who hung himself in their barn. The psychic went on to say that the spirit was not harmful, and with the ongoing renovations to the home, he would eventually no longer consider it to be "his home," and then he would move on.

Though Faith has never actually seen the spirit's apparition, she has seen black shadows out of the corner of her eye that could be attributed to him. She also noticed a dark shadow making an impression on her bed one night as she approached her bedside, but as soon as she hit the light switch, it was gone. Incidents such as these send chills up her spine, she admits, but "it's more the startling of the moment, not the fear."

The couple recently invited PSI, a suave team of investigators, into their home. When the person who interviewed Faith and Jerry was finished, he went outside to let the two who were taking various readings around the premises know that he was done. The three investigators then returned to the house, but the door was locked, even though Jerry remembered double-checking the door before the investigators arrived to make sure it was unlocked for unfettered access around their property. A bit later, when one of the investigators returned for a notepad he had left inside, the door was once again locked. He was as stumped as Jerry and Faith about the incident.

Jerry, who has lived in the house much longer than Faith, remains a non-believer until he receives visual confirmation of a true spirit being on their premises. But Faith has been keeping track of every unexplained incident, and Jerry has yet to find a logical explanation for them.

The Paperboy

Crary Mills

It's a common scene played out across America every morning—the paperboy riding by on his bicycle, smiling and waving to everyone he sees as he tosses their papers onto the front lawn. People respond in kind, waving back when they see him—if they see him. Not everybody sees the paperboy, when he's a ghost.

Though she was only four or five years old at the time, Sue remembers it like it was yesterday, even though it was more than forty years ago. She recalls sitting at the breakfast table in a house on the Post Road and watching the paperboy ride by every morning at the same time. Looking back, she realizes his clothes were a little out of date, being knickers and "those old garters they used to wear on the sleeves of their shirts." The scene was always the same, but it was witnessed only by Sue and her older brother and sister. Their mother saw them wave and heard them say, "Hey, there's the paperboy," but she never saw the boy herself. In fact, where the youngsters saw him would have been difficult to ride a bike, because it was a lawn with a giant hole in it that had been an old well at one time. But Sue insists that the boy "was as solid-looking as you or I" and would always smile and wave back at them.

Sue believes both the house and the land were haunted and gets an eerie feeling recalling her younger years living in the house she now calls "evil."

Her mother once saw mysterious lights coming up out of the ground in the backyard that looked like Roman candles, and the children occasionally saw some type of strange black and white animal by the woods behind the house that they haven't been able to identify to this day. One time they also saw a tiny imp-like man scowling out of the upstairs window at them, causing them all to run away screaming. And Sue's sister saw a man dressed in black standing over her bed one night.

Sue used to dream that the house was on fire. She says, "I was awake, I was sitting straight up on the bed, and I could see the flames shooting up the stairs and smell the smoke and feel the heat. I used to scream until my dad came up and carried me downstairs. I did this a lot when I was younger."

Interestingly, the house burned to the ground after the family moved out, and a mobile home was then moved onto the property. Sue still gets the chills driving by the place and wonders if the new landowners have experienced anything unusual.

The Sessions House

Norfolk

The Sessions House at 1888 Sober Street, Norfolk

It happens all the time—solid, scientific-minded individuals experience something science can't explain, and they are transformed into believers of the paranormal. Ann Sessions has been telling people for years that her pleasant-looking home at 1888 Sober Street was haunted, and the majority of her friends thought she was crazy. What would it take to make them believe her? Surely, if they saw what she has seen, they would change their minds, just as she did in 1995.

Ann's large brick house was built in the early 1800s. The abstract dates back to 1863. She doesn't know a lot about the history of the

89

home, but she has been told by older Norfolk residents that an elderly woman died there, and a younger man committed suicide out back. Maybe those incidents help to explain the many seemingly unexplainable things that have happened to Ann since she has lived there.

One time a snowmobile started up and then turned off completely on its own. Sliding mirror doors—the type used on bedroom closets—have opened right before her eyes. She has seen mysterious points of light swirling up the wall toward the ceiling and a ghostly form glide across her living room at 3 a.m. Footsteps are often heard upstairs when Ann is the only one home. Several friends who have visited have seen and felt the edge of their beds cave down like someone sat on them, but nobody was there.

None of these incidents, however, have felt threatening; so Ann doesn't mind living there. In fact, she's more concerned about intruders coming in from the outside than she is about the intruders from within. So . . . beware of the guard geese!

The Skull

Elizabethtown

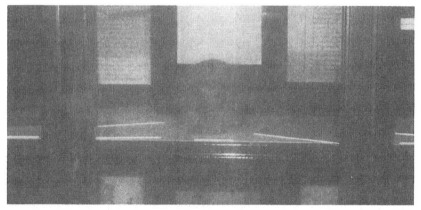

The skull of convicted wife murderer, Henry Debosnys, on display at the Adirondack History Center Museum, Elizabethtown

Jessie Olcott was a first-year intern at the Essex County Historical Society's Adirondack History Center Museum in 2001, when she discovered a twisted coincidence that would change her life. The man whose skull sat in a display case at the museum was hung more than a century earlier with the assistance of her ancestor, Deputy Sheriff S. S. Olcott, much to her surprise. That was disturbing enough for a sensitive young girl to digest. But, imagine her horror when she saw an apparition of the hanged man while putting together the exhibit!

Henry D. Debosnys willingly turned his dead body over to medicine long before it was the fashionable thing to do. However, he didn't do it out of the goodness of his heart—if such a thing even existed in the man. He did it in exchange for a nice new suit to wear to his hanging; and it wasn't so that he would look nice where *he* was going! He probably wanted to impress the many women in the audience with a charming and polished image right to the bitter end. The local doctor offered to fit him with a new suit, if he could have full rights to Mr. Debosnys's soon-to-be lifeless body, so they shook hands and made a deal.

A self-portrait of Henry Debosnys

A little strange, you say? Everything about Essex County's last hanging and the man they hung is peculiar and fraught with mystery—and that's before we even get into the part where he haunts the museum that displays his skull and the noose that hung him.

The 46-year-old Mr. Debosnys claimed that he sailed his own yacht up Lake Champlain from Philadelphia, after being wounded in the Battle at Gettysburg—one of several wars he alleges to have fought in around the world. He then sought work painting or as a farmhand in the Essex County area. I find it odd that a man who could fluently speak and write at least six languages, was a gifted sketch artist, and clearly had above-average intelligence, came all the way to Northern New York merely to paint houses or find farm labor.

More likely, something else drew him to the area—perhaps a newspaper article about a recently widowed woman of considerable means, as some suggested after his death.

In Essex he met and courted the widow, Elizabeth (Betsey) Wells. He bragged to the woman he was intent on marrying that he was a well-traveled, well-educated man, having been born in Portugal and educated in France, before finding his way to the United States. He charmed his way into her life and home. Two months into their marriage—after weeks of arguing with her to put her substantial holdings in his name—he was charged with her brutal murder. Her body was discovered on August 1, 1882, buried under brush on a trail three miles from her residence in Essex. Debosnys had taken her to Port Henry the day before by horse and buggy on the false premise of meeting his father, who was supposedly bringing the couple valuables from France. As they were picnicking by the side of the road, Debosnys snuck up behind her, stabbed her, and then shot her. Neighbors had seen the couple on the trail to Port Henry the day before, but the next day, the same neighbors only saw Debosnys acting strangely in the brush by the side of the trail. They became more suspicious when they saw his empty wagon further down the trail, so they searched the area and came upon Betsey's body. Debosnys was found a short time later that day back at his wife's homestead, with the jewelry she had been wearing in his possession, and was charged with her murder.

Mr. Debosnys was sent to Essex County Jail to await his execution. While in jail, he spent months writing poetry in the fashion of Edgar Allen Poe—dark, demented, brilliant. Twenty-five poems he wrote in all, and they are kept on file at the Adirondack History Center Museum, along with his original sketches, many that shared the theme of his poetry—death. One example follows:

"The City of Death"

Strangers who pass near this grave,
Let awhile your studious eyes engage in your head,

And when returning to your home, you may say,
We have seen the last home, where we have to go and stay.
From which is no return no more, no, no more –
And never feel the splendor of the sun, no more.
They turned their heads, and as he spoke,
A sudden splendor all around them broke.
And they beheld an orb, ample and bright,
Rise from the Holy well, and cast its light,
Round the rich city of the death, and the plain –
Shone out to bless the breaking of the chain
That now sinks beneath an unexpected arm
And in a death-groan, give its last alarm.
Its hand full of joy, proclaim through Heaven
The triumph of its own soul forgiven.
Joy, joy, here forever – my task is done,
The gates of misery are passed, and Heaven's won.
The scene which I have journeyed over –
Return no more – no! no! no more.
This awakes my hourly sighing
Dreary is the thought of dying.
Let me resign a wretched breath
Since now that remain on me
No other calm than kindly death –
To soothe my last trouble, my last misery
But having sworn upon the holy grave
To conquer or perish, once more gave
No less in number and we let them all stay.
Come with me now, I will give my life away
Yes, poor wretched – thine is such a grief
Beyond all hope, all terror, all relief;
And dark, cold calm, which nothing now can break,
Or warm, or brighten, like the water on the lake.
Liberty now for me – would be of a short season,
After my terrible suffering in this poor prison.
Though in my earliest life Bereft –
Lost in that sweet dream, such a change in life
Though hope deceived, pleasure left –
I wish to sigh my latest breath

And go meet my poor wife into death.
To you all, my soul's affections move
My life had burned here like a stove.
If your sorrow faith be over, I will try
To bless you, and your names, and go to die?

Henry D. Debosnys
September 18, 1882 – Essex County Jail

According to a woman whose mother visited Debosnys in jail, when asked what he used for the red coloring in his sketches, he stated that it came from the blood of flies he caught in his cell. His disturbed thinking didn't keep the public away, though. Instead, women filed through the jail continuously, sharing their poetry with the charming and dashing madman who had acquired somewhat of a fan club of admirers. Others stopped by out of curiosity to take notes on his life and to interview the man who was about to be hung. He proclaimed his innocence, both in court and in verse, to the very end—and many who met him, believed him. But his version of the events that led to his wife's murder didn't quite live up to his notable intelligence; there was no doubt that he had been the murderer, when all was said and done.

The case of the scholarly killer was well-known throughout the Northern New York region, drawing a large crowd to witness his hanging on April 27, 1883. Mr. Debosnys smiled out at the crowd, walked calmly up to his spot on the scaffold, looking sharp and nonchalant in his new $15 suit. Moments later, after commenting sarcastically that the rope was a little tight around his neck, he was hung, marking the end of a bizarre episode in Essex County history.

Dr. Pattison, as agreed, took immediate possession of the body, and donated the skeleton to Westport Central School as a learning tool. Eventually, the skeleton fell apart and was disposed of, leaving only the skull in tact. The skull was then donated by the school to the Adirondack History Center, which also acquired other items related to the case that are now on display at the museum. Those items include the actual noose, a pass to the hanging, the original sketches

TO MY poor wife

She died like golden insect in the dew.
Calm and pure; and not a chord was wrong
In her deep heart- but live, she perished young
But perished wasted by some fatal flame
That fed upond her vital, and there came
Death sweeping lightly, like a stream
Along her brain, She perished like a dream!

By her Husband H. DEBOSNYS.

Elizabethtown Essex C° New york
Dec, 12. 1882.

*Henry Debosnys drew this sketch of his wife and wrote the poem
about her death (one of many poems he wrote about death),
while in jail awaiting his hanging for her murder.*

and poetry of the imprisoned man, and correspondence to and from his jail cell.

The man who called himself Henry Deletnack Debosnys was not who he said he was. That name was another fabrication of his twisted mind. To this day, nobody has figured out exactly who he was or what his true life story was. Though he sketched elaborate estates and castles that he claimed to have lived in abroad, and he told of a devout and prominent upbringing, no evidence has ever been found to tie his name into the places he claimed to have been. In fact, one of the towns he said his family lived in doesn't even exist—at least not today. No mention of the surname he created for himself can be found either, not even on the internet.

One shelf of the Debosnys exhibit, showing the noose that hung him, along with original poetry and sketches he created while imprisoned

He admitted that he would prevent his real family, which included at least one son, from ever being shamed by learning of his fate. The scholarly linguist who created an indecipherable pictographic alphabet similar to hieroglyphics took all of his many secrets to the grave with him, but the evidence of his dark genius remains—locked away in file cabinets and in a glass display case at the museum.

An example of the pictographic alphabet Debosnys sometimes wrote with. It has never been deciphered.

Jessie's first encounter with the ghost of Henry Debosnys occurred when she first started working as an intern at the museum, before she even knew who he was or what he had done. She said it happened in the museum's Brewster Library when the copier apparently ran a copy by mysterious means. When the employees first arrived that morning, they found a photocopy of a newspaper article in the out tray of the copier, but there was nothing in the copier from which to make the copy! It was a copy of an old newspaper clipping dated May 3, 1883, about the trial and execution of Mr. Debosnys. When they held up the copy to ask the other staff in the library if anyone had copied it, they all said they hadn't; and at that same moment, the power went out in the building and surrounding area.

The full meaning of the incident hadn't hit any of them yet. But it certainly got Jessie's attention. As she read the article, she noticed that an Olcott ancestor had assisted with the hanging. That was rather disturbing, but she couldn't resist the temptation to find out all she could about the Debosnys case, and she set about passionately creating an exhibit on the case. Little did she know that she might get more than she bargained for.

Once when Jessie and another intern were in the basement doing a bulk mailing, the other girl noticed a face in the glass of a table on the floor below. Jessie saw it, too, after the girl pointed it out to her. Both girls said hello, but nobody answered. It was odd, because nobody had walked by them. So they went upstairs to get Margaret Gibbs, director of the museum and their boss. The three women searched the building thoroughly for the person whose face was seen just moments before, but they found nobody. It was admittedly strange, but nobody would lose any sleep over it just yet.

Then one night after researching the Debosnys newspaper articles, Jessie had a dream that she was locked in the Brewster Library, and people were coming out of the walls at her. She was screaming for someone to let her out when a girl with a long blue skirt and shirt with stripes and a red thing around her neck touched her arm and told her it would be okay. But it felt so real that Jessie woke up. The next day at the museum, she found a box with Mr. Debosnys' poems and sketches in it. Among the documents was a sketch of three girls next to the grave of Elizabeth; they were three of her four daughters. Jessie immediately sensed that the youngest girl was the one in her dream, yet she still never thought anything paranormal was going on.

Another day, while Jessie was working on the Debosnys exhibit, two women from Rochester came in. They were descendants of Elizabeth Wells, and they had come to do some research on Debosnys and his trial. Coincidentally, Jessie happened to have all of the documents and items for the exhibit laid out nicely on the large library tables, so the timing of their visit couldn't have been better. They told Jessie they didn't feel right about having Debosnys glorified with an exhibit, but she explained that her interest in the case was because she was a descendant of one of the people who led him to the gallows, and they understood that.

The women tried to take a couple of photographs of the skull, but the camera suddenly stopped working after the first photograph. But the women got the information they were after, and before leaving, they told Jessie where Elizabeth was buried so she could include a photograph of the woman's grave in the museum's files. When the interns drove to the gravesite, they found Elizabeth's grave in a shady area and snapped a picture with Jessie's mother's brand new camera. Just as they snapped it, however, the camera broke. When Jessie's mother got the film developed, every picture on the role came out, except the picture of Elizabeth's grave. Luckily, the negative turned out, so they were able to get the photograph off the negative. Jessie said the picture shows anomalous spots of light on it, even though there was no sunlight around the grave. It, too, can be viewed at the museum.

By now, Jessie was quite spooked by all of the unexplained incidents since she had begun delving into the Debosnys case. The final incident occurred as Jessie was turning off the upstairs lights in the breaker panel. The switches in the cabinet have to be turned off one by one, but before she'd even flicked the first switch, they all went off rapidly, one by one, on their own! Margaret heard her yell and came running. She tried the switches, and they were working normally. But she'd been right there out in the hallway when she heard them go off almost instantaneously, like going down through the panel of switches at a superhuman speed. That was the most disturbing incident that occurred; and, thankfully, it was the last.

Since the exhibit opened, there have been no further unexplained occurrences. The skull is locked securely inside an attractive display case. Looking at it, you can't help but think about the brain that was once enclosed in that skull—and the many secrets that it took with it to the grave. Secrets yet to be unraveled.

The Tilden Stage Inn

Lisbon

Tilden Stage as seen from Route 37, Lisbon

Deatta Youngs lived at Tilden Stage before it became the inviting inn that it is today. In 1990, the 160-year-old home was rented out as a one-family dwelling, while plans for renovating it into a bed and breakfast were finalized. An interesting thing about the house, Deatta noted, was that it sometimes seemed to fix itself – repairs that were needed were done right under her nose. She never saw, nor heard, anyone fixing the things that needed repair and nobody admitted to doing it. But it was fine with Deatta. She was pregnant at the time, and, rather than being afraid by the "Mr. Fix-It" incidents, she recalls feeling like someone was simply helping her out.

When Deatta noticed that one of the cellar windows was out, she kept saying, "We've got to fix that window." About a week later, she went down in the basement and found it was fixed! They never found out who fixed it, or how, or when.

Another time, a broken door handle was mysteriously repaired. Although Deatta rented the entire house, she kept the upstairs closed off, because she already had plenty of room in the huge place. However, the few times Deatta did venture upstairs, she had to put the broken door handle in and work it just right, because it was not attached to the door. One time she went up and, without thinking, she automatically pulled at the door handle to open it, but the door handle fell off. The next time she went upstairs, the handle had been properly and permanently fixed to the door! Once again, nobody took credit for doing it.

Unexplained repair jobs were not the only thing the tenants found perplexing. Footsteps were often heard and, in one case, actually *seen* in the dust on the floor upstairs. Deatta explained that there was always a lot of pitter-patter around the place, but one time when she went upstairs, she and several other people saw a single footprint in the dust. It was the left bare foot of a small child, and there was no small child in their home. The footsteps of a larger person, perhaps wearing boots, were sometimes heard during the night going through the house, up the stairs, and into the closet. After the sound of the closet door closing, there would be silence, like whomever it was intended to stay in the closet. The next morning, Deatta or her son would go upstairs and find no footprints other than their own in the dust; and the latch to the closet door would be undone, even though they had closed it securely the last time they'd investigated the strange sound of footsteps.

There was also a time when Deatta's mother came to visit, and she was taking her mother out for a bit. Since there are four doors to get out of the house, she left one light on so that if they returned after dark, they could still see to get in the house. Then she locked all four doors, as she always did. When they returned home that evening, every single one of the doors was wide open.

Another morning when Deatta's mother was visiting, the woman asked her daughter why someone was crawling across the floor all night. She said it sounded like someone crawling across the floor on their butt, the way she had to for a short time after her accident. She asked if it might have been Chris, her granddaughter's friend, but Deatta explained that he had been sleeping on the living room floor beside the futon bed that Deatta so often slept in before she had the house fully furnished. He slept there because he was too afraid to sleep elsewhere, having heard too many things himself during his many visits to the house.

One day, Deatta got an awful migraine just as she was about to take her daughter, Rebecca, to dance class. Her husband told her to lie down and he would take their daughter and would be right back. Deatta got back up and said, "I'll go and lock the door." But then she changed her mind and said, "No, I won't lock it, because then I'd have to get up when you get home and go unlock it." When he came back home, the door was locked, so Deatta ended up having to get up anyway. It should be no surprise to anyone by now that doors are one of ghosts' favorite objects to manipulate.

Chris Smith of Lisbon was one of Rebecca's best friends. He spent a lot of time at their home, but he admits he wasn't always crazy about being there. He heard "lots of things, like running around upstairs." He heard the upstairs closet door open, then slam shut in the night, just as Deatta and her son did. The next day he, too, would find the door wide open. One night, he said, "There was Becca and me and another person in there, and Becca went to her room, and the other person was somewhere else, and I was sitting there and the basement door opened up. So I shut it, but it just kept opening; so, automatically, I assumed the latch was broken, and I went over and shut the thing. That's when it swung wide open against the wall, and that was it." Someone was determined to get the last word in.

Speaking of words, Chris heard unexplained, incoherent voices one or two times, but Rebecca heard someone calling her name when she was alone there after school. She couldn't tell if it was male or female, but it's possible it was her grandmother's ex-boyfriend who had passed away when she was younger. She had been very fond of the man, named Cy. She was afraid to go in the house before her mother got home after school, because she once saw Cy's face in the television. Or, if the television was turned off, all of a sudden, it would go on by itself. One night Rebecca woke up crying and told her mother she had seen Cy up on the dresser. After crying for a long time, she finally admitted to her mother how much she loved Cy and missed him. Then the appearances stopped. Cy had been making his visitations to help Rebecca work through her grief. Once she had, his job was done.

Deatta and her family lived in the house from 1990 through 1991. They moved out during renovations for the bed and breakfast. During that time, they were visited by a small, barefoot ghost and a male ghost who sounded like he was wearing boots. Cy also visited them, as a concerned spirit, and then he moved on. Whether the other two ghosts remain there is not known. But if they are still there, they certainly are well-mannered. One obligingly fixes things and the other takes his shoes off before he comes in!

Turn Around

Massena

Photo by author

Entrance gate to the Pine Grove Cemetery, Massena

Like many people, Joan Szarka has always been intrigued by cemeteries. She and her son, Blake, often strolled through the shaded Pine Grove Cemetery in their neighborhood, reading the stones with interest and discussing them. But all that changed after "the incident." Joan has not been back to the cemetery since the evening a phantom crept up behind her and ordered her to "turn around."

The Pine Grove Cemetery Association created the cemetery, with its winding, paved paths, on Beach Street in 1872, for Massena's five hundred residents of that time. Of course, once industry came to Massena and the population explosion occurred, Pine Grove quickly filled its original 486 lots. One of the people buried at the cemetery, before its expansion, was Dragon Obretenoff. The unusual name on the tombstone grabbed Joan's attention as she was walked by it one day. It's a plain, red granite stone that simply states the name and the years of birth and death, 1897-1949. The plot, to the left of the mausoleum, sits on a downhill slope just off the furthest road at the back of the cemetery, with the dense treeline as its backdrop. The untended grave seemed lonely to Joan the first time she saw it, and she said, "It just seemed to speak to me." She meant, of course, that it drew her attention toward it; but it wouldn't be long before her words, taken literally, would become a reality.

Photo by author

The tombstone of Dragon Obretenoff

Joan was curious about this Dragon guy, and, after asking around, she discovered that he had been shot and killed. She assumed that meant that he had been murdered, but she didn't know the details of his tragic death. Joan and Blake spoke kindly of the man each time they passed by his lonely grave on their evening walks through the grounds.

One summer evening, Joan, Blake, and Blake's dog, Sport, walked through the gated archway into the cemetery and perceived a distinct change in temperature. It was noticeably colder in the cemetery than on the street just outside the gate, and there seemed to be "a vibe" everywhere they walked. Joan and her son are both quite sensitive to subtleties around them of that nature. Joan said, "The full moon was playing peek-a-boo with some clouds and casting shadows." But it was still a beautiful night, and they had walked through the peaceful cemetery many times before, so they really thought nothing more of it. They continued walking their usual route through the graveyard, and when they came to Dragon's stone, they found themselves talking about what the circumstances of his death might have been. They wondered what happened and why.

Just then, as they were discussing Dragon's fate, Sport began acting strangely. The dog pulled away from Blake and started to whine. The wind seemed to pick up, and the dog became even more unsettled. Blake felt a chill go straight through him and thought he saw an apparition at the same instant. That was when Joan heard it. A raspy whisper—slow and deliberate—told her to turn around. Joan shuddered and picked up her gait, as they made haste toward the exit. She nervously asked her son if he had heard what she had. He nodded.

Photo by author
"The incident" took place as Joan and Blake walked down this path.

At the time, Joan and Blake believed that the chilling command must have had something to do with Dragon's death. They thought that perhaps those were the last words he'd ever heard, but they still didn't know the circumstances surrounding his death. An old *Massena Observer* newspaper article Joan found, however, finally shed some light on the mystery. It stated that Dragon had been shot in a hunting accident on November 21, 1949, in the Town of Madrid. He was hunting alone when another hunter said he saw something moving in the brush and mistook it for a deer. Dragon was shot in the face and chest and mortally wounded. The coroner ruled the death accidental, and that was the end of that, and the end of Dragon.

He had been a well-known local restaurateur who owned Wimpy's Diner and was co-owner of the Pine Grove Restaurant. Though he was born in Bulgaria and had traveled the world, he finally settled in Massena, where he lived to be fifty-two. His gravestone was lonely and untended, because he never married and had no relatives locally, as most of his family remained in Bulgaria. But Dragon was very fond of Massena. During his acceptance speech as president of his class at the Massena Naturalization School in 1939, he said, "I have been all over the world and have seen some beautiful places, but America is the best, especially right here in Massena. I intend to make my home here for the rest of my life." That would only be ten more years.

Now Joan questions if the chilling words she heard that night had anything to do with Dragon, after all. Perhaps he simply wanted to meet her—he was known to be quite the womanizer—and she had shown an interest in him, with the way she'd been asking around about him and talking about him. Maybe he just wanted her to meet him face to face, so he told her to turn around.

Or maybe the specter that brushed past Blake and told Joan to turn around was from an entirely different stone and had nothing whatsoever to do with Dragon, even though he's the one they were talking about at the moment the disturbing incident took place. Speculation goes hand in hand with matters of a paranormal nature.

Regardless of the explanation, Joan and Blake probably won't be going by Dragon's gravesite any time soon. But if you do, say a prayer for Old Dragon. And say a prayer that you never hear the words, "turn around," as you're strolling through the Pine Grove Cemetery on some balmy, summer evening.

We Love You, Mary

Ogdensburg

Chris Sharlow is no stranger to ghost stories, having experienced many of his own. It takes quite a lot to rattle him these days. But the following story, told to him by a good friend whose grandmother lived in a haunted house, can't be repeated without shuddering.

Mary lived in an apartment complex in Ogdensburg which supposedly was swamp land before the complex was built. The rumor was that it had been an ancient Indian burial or ceremonial ground that was later a dumping ground for the unfortunate victims of the Mafia's hold on Ogdensburg during Prohibition.

Mary was "a lady of strong faith in her Catholic beliefs," and her apartment was adorned with statues of Christ and the Virgin Mary, ensuring protection against all evil. Chris said, "I believe these objects of faith helped her defeat an unusually malevolent presence in her home."

Chris' friend said that Mary had experienced strange incidents such as seeing shadows slinking along the walls throughout the apartment and hearing whispers, even though she lived there alone. She believed the shadows were evil entities, because they tormented her daily. She began tossing holy water into the corners of her apartment and watched incredulously as the shadows that usually cowered in the corners leapt out of the way to avoid being hit. It took everything she had to round the entities up by sprinkling holy water and chanting prayers as she made her way down the stairs and straight out the front door.

On one particular day, Mary knew she was winning the battle when she heard the manipulative shadows speak, as they scurried down the stairs with the holy water splashing at their backs. They said, "We love you, Mary. We love you, Mary. We love you, Mary." It was as if they were trying to win her over, like a child begging for a toy. But when they realized their attempts had proven futile, they began saying, "We *hate* you, Mary. We *hate* you, Mary." Then, with the slam of the front door, they were gone.

Chris said one thing he's learned is that, "the stronger your faith and conviction is toward God, the more you may be bombarded by evil as it tries to shake your faith." And if a little old woman armed only with holy water and prayer can banish evil, so can anyone.

PART II

Spirit Encounters
with Loved Ones

.

A Gift Straight From Heaven

Massena

When Heather and her father returned from an overnight trip to Watertown last year to visit her sister, her father heard a cat meowing just as he got out of the car. They walked into his garage and found a tiny orange kitten sitting on his three-wheeler.

Heather's mother had an orange cat named Slinker when she was very young, but when her family moved from North Bangor to Massena, her father told her she had to leave the cat behind. Of course, she was heartbroken. However, about two months later, Slinker showed up on their doorstep on Hubbard Road—somehow having found its way to their new home, as cats incredibly do. After all that the poor cat had been through to be reunited with its family, Heather's grandfather felt he had no choice but to let his daughter keep it.

Several days before she was unexpectedly stricken last year, Heather's mother decided she wanted a kitten just like her old Slinker. She never saw her wish granted, at least not from an earthly vantage point; but it was granted nonetheless—to her unsuspecting husband. Lo and behold, a tiny orange kitten exactly like a miniature Slinker showed up mysteriously in their garage, just days after the funeral, and it acted like it belonged there. Did Heather's mom have something to do with it? There's no way to be sure, but she always said she would let her family know she was around after she died.

Heather said her father still has the kitten which gives him good company, as well as a reason to get up and get moving each day, because somebody has to feed and pet her. Oddly enough, the kitten has this new habit of playing with the typewriter. Heather's mother was a proficient typist and always used her typewriter for correspondence. Another coincidence? I think not.

It seems as if Heather's mother found a perfect way to show her family she's okay now and is still with them in spirit. The kitten brought comfort and joy to one family in their time of need. It truly is a gift straight from Heaven.

Get Out Now!

Ogdensburg

Frances Morrison will never forget the night their underground barn caught fire and was totally destroyed. She and her husband, Carl, and their sons were in the stable letting out their cattle. Frances could see the flames overhead as she let out ten more cows. She knew the tractor was right above her in the hayloft. Suddenly, a very loud, distinct male voice said, "Get out and get out *now!*" She knew it wasn't her husband or sons—it didn't sound at all like them, and it literally seemed to come from someone "up there." She also knew that she shouldn't get out yet, no matter *who* was telling her to. There were still at least thirty more head of cattle to save. Carl and Robert let out ten heifers and the bull, and then they all made a run for it. Just as Frances exited, the barn collapsed, but she and her family were all safe. That was in 1975.

Fifteen years later, Frances once again encountered someone from "up there" in the same home at 707 Pray Road. In 1990, Ogdensburg obstetrician Dr. Joseph Brandy and his family died tragically in a plane crash. Frances and Carl purchased some of the doctor's belongings at an auction shortly after the tragedy: an antique bed, some bedding, some pictures, and so on. As they unloaded the items into their living room on that same day, Frances happened to glance into the kitchen, and standing there by the freezer was the likeness of Dr. Brandy! He was dressed very nicely in a brown suit and a white shirt with a silk tie, and he was smiling. She believes the doctor was telling her he was happy they had his things and that he was okay.

The Morrison family has lived in the old house since 1904, and

Frances has lived there for forty-one years. She has heard a story about a dead nurse haunting the house, but she has never personally encountered that particular ghost, although she has noticed shadows out of the corner of her eye on more than one occasion. What she mainly sees are spirits that are known to her, with the exception of the one acting as her guardian that night in the barn fire. Besides Dr. Brandy's single appearance, she strongly believes that her son, Robert, who was murdered in 1993 at the age of twenty-nine, visits their home quite frequently.

Shortly after Robert's funeral, his sister Sara felt him go by her bed. Then her son Steven's wife, Michelle, thought it was their cat Peeper and shooed him away, but Steve said, "It's just Rob. Go to sleep." The whole family has become quite accustomed to Robert's presence in their earthy lives. Frances was not at all surprised to hear Carl describe how he sat listening to Robert walking back and forth overhead one day. It was as if he was looking for something up in his old bedroom.

Another time Frances was awakened by the sound of someone running between her and Carl's bed and dresser, but she couldn't open her eyes quickly enough to catch whoever it was in the act. When she finally got her eyes working, she saw that the ears of her three cats were back, as if the felines had been spooked. She has felt a hand on her shoulder when nobody was there, and she has heard someone walking around the table—presumably Robert. Family members also smell toast when nobody has made any, and nobody has been home.

There is a silver Christmas bell that Frances bought when Carl was in the hospital in Glens Falls one year. She loved it, and it was always the first item she brought out at Christmas time. However, Robert couldn't understand why his mother was so fond of it or why it seemed special, so he more or less ignored it. But the day after Christmas in 2002, Frances and Carl heard the bell ring early in the morning all by itself, while everyone was still in bed. That was a unique way for Robert to greet them, Frances said, because he hated that bell and would never have rung it while he was alive, unless he really wanted to prove his love for them.

It just goes to show you, love overcomes all obstacles...even in death.

Help From Beyond

Pyrites

Ceylon Brabaw was not afraid to die. He and Kelly, his wife of twenty years, spoke openly about the subject, because they knew his time here on earth was questionable, due to a heart condition. He assured Kelly that when he reached the other side, he would somehow contact her. After all, the two had been inseparable, according to Kelly. Theirs was a truly magical relationship; one that would surely carry over into the afterlife. Ceylon died very suddenly in August 2000, and—true to his word—he would soon find several ways to contact his wife.

Less than a week after he died, Kelly was lying in bed feeling very lonely and sad when she felt "the softest, sweetest breeze" brush across her face. None of the windows were open. She immediately felt calm and serene and told Ceylon that she knew he was there, she loved him, and she would be okay. She believes it was his way of letting her know that he, too, was okay.

Kelly has since remarried—she is now Kelly Jacoby of Pyrites—but she still feels her first husband's presence once in a while, as if he's checking in on her for a brief moment. During those times, she whispers that she knows he's there and that she loves him.

As far as the magical moments that characterized their relationship, Ceylon still had another trick up his sleeve. He made two commode doors appear out of thin air earlier this year. Kelly had an old antique commode that she wanted to get refinished, but Ceylon had removed the two doors years ago so that Kelly could use it to display her chamber pots in. There was no sense getting the piece refinished without the original doors, she felt, but she was sure Ceylon had thrown them out or burned them. She knew they weren't in the cellar, because she had emptied it out entirely when her new husband moved in.

Well, they say Christmas is made for surprises, and during the holiday season of 2002-2003, Kelly got the surprise of her life. She had gone down cellar to get something, when she saw—there at the bottom of the stairs, smack in the middle of the floor—the two original, beat-up commode doors. She has no doubt that it was Ceylon's holiday surprise for her.

Little Did She Know

Fort Covington

Rhonda was awakened one night when she felt a very cold hand on the side of her face. She glanced toward the clock on her nightstand, but her view was blocked by something she couldn't see. At the same time that her clock finally came back into view, she noticed a black form gliding from the room. It was 4:15 a.m.—the exact time her husband had passed away two weeks before.

Rhonda and her husband lived in an old house on Water Street at the time of his passing in 1983. He died at the age of forty, after two weeks in a coma following an automobile accident. The following year, Rhonda and their daughter moved into the house the couple had been planning to build on the Burns-Holden Road. It was poignant moving on like that, knowing that her husband wouldn't be able to join them as the family continued with the plans he had set in motion. He must have been able to sense her emotional dilemma, because within a week of moving into their new home, Rhonda's teenage daughter announced that she could hear her father's distinctive walk up and down the hallway at night.

Some may find the presence of a deceased loved one's spirit comforting, but many perceive it as strange and frightening, even though they know who it is. Having never experienced such a thing to know how I would feel in the same situation, I can't say that I blame them. Rhonda's daughter was "petrified," and she moved out of the home as soon as she turned sixteen.

Rhonda often heard her husband's voice, and he once told her to call a friend because the friend was "in need." The following day, she did as told and learned that the friend's mother had died. It was eerie, to say the least. Nobody believed her when she told them the things that had transpired since her husband died. In fact, they told her she was crazy.

When confronted with information they don't understand, some people make insensitive remarks, like those that Rhonda endured—until the day something unexplained happens to them. Indeed, Rhonda herself was a skeptic, but she now admits, "Little did I understand until it happened to me." She has moved from the house on the Burns-Holden Road, and it seems her husband has finally moved on as well, for she no longer hears his voice or senses his presence. He must be at peace.

Nothing Is Impossible

North Lawrence

Georgianne "Georgi" Muench is a gifted channeler who lives in North Lawrence and helps those seeking answers from beyond. She has learned that nothing is impossible. This is her story, in her own words:

"About eleven or twelve years ago, I opened myself through meditation, practice, and—most of all—faith, to become a communicator between the living and those who have passed over. . . . The spiritual energy of one of those who has passed over asked me to relay the story of our communication.

"He was a young boy that I had met once or twice before he had passed, although I do not need to meet a person in life to communicate with them after their death. He was killed in a tragic vehicular accident. I had not yet heard the news by way of radio or other earthly means of receiving such information. The night before the news was broadcast on the radio, I had a dream of this boy. He came to me and told me of his passing. I assumed it was just a dream as I had never, up to that point, been made aware of a person's passing in this manner. The radio confirmed my dream early the next morning.

"Later that day, the boy came to me and asked if I would go to the services his family was having for him to let his mother know that he was all right. I was not comfortable approaching his mother at that time, because I know from my own experience of loss how difficult it is to cope at that time. I asked him to bring his mother to me when she would be ready to know and hear the things he needed me to communicate to her.

"I heard nothing from his mother for weeks after his passing and each time he asked me to pursue it, I reminded him of my request to get her to me, rather than me getting to her. Months passed and I began to relax about his request; my nervousness subsided. Then one day, out of the blue, the phone rang. When I answered it, to my surprise, it was his mother. She had a question for me. It was connected to my profession, but the question was really not directed towards my field. That made me realize it was him getting her to me. While I was talking to her, her son was dancing around the room laughing and saying, 'I got her to contact you, please tell her,' and he kept repeating it. At that point, I knew I had to tell her of my abilities and the message from her son.

"I interrupted our conversation and began to explain that I had information from her son who had passed over. He told her he was fine and happy and his passing was not an accident. He needed to be on the other side to do the work he had to do for those that remained here, alive. He gave her several pieces of information to validate that he was, indeed, the one giving her those messages. I am sure it was difficult for her to hear his words, as she cried when she realized he was still with her. We spoke for several hours that day, so he could relay all that he needed her to know and understand. She was very open and receptive to the information, especially when he validated his existence.

"Since then, he has communicated many times through me to her and has begun to communicate directly to her. At this writing, he has communicated the importance of relating the existence of the spiritual energy of those who have passed over. We don't lose our loved ones when they die, we just change the way of realizing them there."

Out of the Mouths of Babes

Canton

Children say it the way they see it, and they see it a lot better than adults. I'm referring to a child's sixth sense—the inherent sense most of us adults have repressed. Children often communicate with unseen people believed to be "imaginary friends." Very often, however, upon further questioning, children can provide details of their so-called imaginary friends that match deceased loved ones the children have never even met (grandparents, great-grandparents, etc.). The children know their names and recognize them in old family photo albums without ever having been told or shown the information.

The following true story was a runner-up in a writing contest sponsored by North Country Public Radio last year. It was written by Logan Thomas Patnode of Cranberry Lake and is being shared with the permission of his mother, Susan Smith.

When I was three years old, my parents got divorced, and my mom, brother, and I were forced to move into a really small house on a street called Mechanic Street. That wasn't too bad, except that I didn't get to see my dad very often. The little house was yellow with green shutters. When you walked into the front door, you were in the living room. To the left of the living room, the bathroom made a halfway wall that separated the living room and the kitchen. That was a pretty interesting corner.

We had lived in the house for a few months when I began doing something a little strange. It was about seven o'clock one night when I did it for the first time. I would stand looking in the corner by the bathroom. "Hi," I said. Then I turned to my mom, who was sitting on the couch, and asked, "Mom? Who's that man standing in the corner?" She was reading and plainly not really paying attention.

"I don't know," she replied.

I knew she wasn't paying attention and decided not to question her further. I just stood there staring at the corner. Every night I would stand in the corner, staring at the wall. And every night I would ask my mom, "Who's that man standing in the corner?" And every night, she would reply, "I don't know." This went on for a few weeks before she got tired of it.

"Mom?" I asked. "Who's that man standing in the corner?"

"Logan," she said, "there's no one standing in the corner."

"Then how come I can see him?" I asked.

"Alright, what does he look like?" she asked sarcastically.

"He's real tall and has a big nose and ears. And he doesn't have a lot of hair, but it's gray," I replied. She just looked at me and then into the corner and then at me again. Then she went back to reading. Every once in a while she would look into the corner again.

"We're going to Grandma's," my mom said one day. We went to Grandma's every once in awhile. I think she helped my mom cope with the divorce. It was a two-hour drive, and when we got there, we had dinner. After dinner Mom talked to Grandma in the living room, while Grandpa, my brother, and I looked at old photo albums in the dining room. When we came to an old black and white photo of the family, I grabbed the album and ran into the living room, shouting, "Mom! Mom!"

When I showed her the picture, I said, "That's the man in the corner!"

"Who is it?" my grandma asked. Mom showed her the picture, and they both stared wide-eyed at it. Evidently, Grandma had heard the entire story.

The next morning, we started for home, and that night I said, "Mom, the man is here again."

She looked in the corner, then said, "Ask him what he wants."

"What do you want?" I asked the wall. After a few seconds, I turned to my mom again. "He wants to know if you're alright."

She sat back. When she sat forward again, there were tears in her eyes. "Tell him yes," she said.

"She said yes," I told him. I turned to face her and said, "Mom, he's gone." She started crying.

It turns out that the man I saw was her grandfather. He died before I was born, and I had never seen a picture of him, though I described him perfectly. I never saw him again after that night, though I looked for him many times. My mom always seemed better about the divorce after that, and I was glad that he and I were there to help.

Phone Call From Beyond

Malone

Brian's grandmother—a strong-willed woman with a passion for life and family—passed away in March of 2000 at 91 years of age. She'd had a stroke three months earlier that left her paralyzed and unable to speak. But once she passed over, there was nothing that could stop her from keeping "in touch."

After his grandmother's wake and funeral, Brian's mother and sisters cleaned out her apartment and divided up the furniture. His mother got the bedroom set, but she didn't have room in her house for it, so she gave it to Brian to keep in the spare bedroom at his house in Massena. Shortly thereafter, Brian and his wife, Marissa, started feeling cold spots all around their house, but especially in the bedroom where his grandmother's bedroom set was. Even in the early summer, the room was very cold. Brian said, "The cold spots seemed to follow us around the house wherever we went." He and Marissa didn't know whether to laugh or cry at the oddity.

An outgoing telephone call helped Marissa decide. She was dialing a phone number, when she was interrupted half-way through by a voice on the other end of the line. Brian heard her say, "No, I didn't." And then she paused for a second and slammed the phone down, "crying as if she was scared to death." She told Brian that she heard a voice on the other end of the line ask her if she saw a dead deer on the side of the road, and when she said, "No, I didn't," the voice said, "You mean, you didn't see the dead deer on the side of the road when you were going to work this morning?" She *had* seen a dead deer, but it was in an area where nobody else could have seen her, because she was the only one there—unless the trees have eyes.

129

When she calmed down a bit, she told Brian that the voice sounded exactly like his grandmother who had just passed away—and whose bedroom set they now possessed. Maybe the old woman wanted to let them know that even though she had died, she was still watching over them from beyond.

When Brian and Marissa moved to Malone later that year, the familiar cold spot near the bedroom set stayed with them, even into their new home. They still feel like they are being followed throughout the house sometimes, and they occasionally feel a hand on their shoulders or a cold hand touching their own. Brian said there are times when they go upstairs, and it looks as if his grandmother is standing at the top—but it's only a fleeting glimpse; just enough to make them wonder if they really saw what they think they saw.

Just recently, Brian's mother and her sister from New Hampshire visited their home. Brian's aunt was curious about the presence that had been felt in the house. The four of them went into the bedroom where his grandmother's bedroom set was, and Brian said, "After about two or three minutes, there was a very strong presence in the room, seeming to move about as if to touch each of us." He said the presence in the spare bedroom felt welcoming, not scary.

The visits from Brian's grandmother have lessened, but he and Marissa believe it's because she understands that her family is doing okay without her. And his grandmother hasn't called Marissa back, but with the price of long distance these days, who can blame her?

Time Heals All Wounds

Canton

*Kimberley Trombley's father, as he
appeared to her after his death*

Kimberley Trombley's father knew what it was to suffer. Before his death in 1997, he had been ill with diabetes, lost his vision and both legs, and had been receiving dialysis. For an active man who enjoyed bowling, gardening, hunting, fishing, and snowmobiling, it was very difficult to give up all of the things he loved doing. The man who raised five fine daughters and served his country in the Air Force for twenty years deserved better. Much better.

Kimberley was the eldest of the sisters. Her relationship with her father while growing up was sometimes turbulent; but, for the most part, they enjoyed each other's company and spent time together going to St. Lawrence University hockey games, snowmobiling, and watching the Islanders on TV. Over the years, they became closer and closer, especially after the birth of Kimberley's daughter. As the circle of life goes, one life had come into the world—into their family—and another life would soon be leaving. It was the best of times and the worst of times.

Kimberley's father died on December 8, the funeral was held at the funeral home, then everyone went to Fairview Cemetery for a 21-gun salute. The body was placed in the vault for a spring burial. A couple of weeks after the funeral, Kimberley felt a strong urge to go to the cemetery. She drove in and pulled up in front of the vault, and she sat there and cried. After what seemed like a very long time, she slowly raised her head and looked in the rear view mirror. To her astonishment, her father was standing behind her car, waving at her. He was standing on the legs he had once had and was wearing his military uniform. He looked as if he had never been sick—as healthy and strong as he was while Kimberley was growing up. In the course of infinity, time heals all wounds.

Kimberley feels her father was telling her to move on with her life. He was okay and would watch over her. The man who had lived such an exemplary life got what he deserved in the end, after all—eternal good health, happiness, and peace. And he returned just long enough to show his daughter that we are immortal beings, and we go on after we die.

The spirit of Kimberley's father, along with so many others, reminds us with greater and greater frequency these days that there's no finality in death—there's only change. And change is good.

Resources

http://www.iroquoisfarm.com

http://www.morleygristmill.com

http://www.neighborsofwatertown.com

http://www.wellscroftlodge.com

Lake Champlain Weekly, May 16, 2001

Mountain Laurel, August 9, 1973

Ogdensburg Advance, July 5, 1917

St. Lawrence Weekly Democrat, July 5, 1917

The Massena Observer, November 29, 1949

Watertown Daily Times, November 4, 2002

"Adirondack History Center Museum" brochure

Documents, including Henry Debosnys's original poems and sketches, from files at the Adirondack History Center Museum

Personal correspondence from the Robert F. Hall Papers collection at the New York State Library, Albany

Various old, unidentifiable newspaper clippings from Burlington and Elizabethtown areas, dated March and April 1883

About the Author

Photo by Creative Imaging

Cheri Revai graduated from Canton College of Technology in 1984 with a degree in Secretarial Science and has been a full-time secretary since then. She was born and raised in Northern New York and lives in the North Country with her husband, Joe, and their four daughters: Michelle, Jamie, Katie, and Nicole.

Cheri's first book, *Haunted Northern New York*, has been a best-seller. Writing non-fiction is a hobby she savors "on the side," when time permits.

You may write to the author at P.O. Box 295, Massena, New York 13662. Or send e-mail to: hauntedny@yahoo.com. The "Haunted Northern New York" companion website is http://www.hauntedny.com.